SO-BFC-225

4.63

Who's Who in Jane Austen and the Brontës

Who's Who
in Jane Austen
and the Brontës

GLENDA LEEMING

TAPLINGER PUBLISHING CO., INC.

NEW YORK

828.03

First published in the United States in 1974 by
TAPLINGER PUBLISHING CO., INC.
New York, New York

Copyright © 1974 by Glenda Leeming
All rights reserved
Printed in Great Britain

No part of this book may be reproduced or transmitted in any form or by any means, electronic or mechanical, including photocopy, recording, or any information storage and retrieval system now known or to be invented, without permission in writing from the publisher, except by a reviewer who wishes to quote brief passages in connection with a review written for inclusion in a magazine, newspaper or broadcast.

Library of Congress Catalog Card Number: 73-17674

ISBN 0-8008-8267-9

Contents

105100

Foreword

This is a really intelligent and useful little book. It gives first a comprehensive and accurate list of all the characters created by Jane Austen, and then a comprehensive and accurate list of all the characters created by the three Brontë sisters.

Their names are alphabetically arranged, with the title of the novel in which they figure added in sensible italics: such a boon for quick reference. Each note gives the person's identity, something of their appearance and a succinct account of their part in the story. Best of all, the notes present vividly their characters, their personalities. A nice tinge of irony, a very neat use of the novelists' own words, a brevity decidedly marked by wit, make these notes pleasurable reading. The items on the horrid Mrs. Norris, on Mrs. Elton, on the abominable Ginevra or the 'kindly but trite' Mrs. Fairfax, are typical specimens.

A very striking point, I think, which adds to our knowledge and understanding of the authors concerned, is almost casually made. When we read the works of these great novelists, we feel that their worlds are very real, full of living people clustering about the main protagonists as they play out their amusing, romantic or tragic stories. Here this impression, perhaps previously vague, is strongly confirmed when we see the appended list of characters book by book. What a number of minor characters there are for our delight! From dear Miss Bates to Bessy the nursemaid, from sailor William Price to the blotchy Sir Thomas Ashby, they are all here, and in the biographical notes they appear in their habit as they lived. What a variety! How true to life!

Rather charmingly, too, a list of our author's *animal* characters is added. Only one, a genteel pointer, figures in Jane's novels, but a couple of pages of horses and dogs appear for the moorland Haworth girls.

Libraries, students and eager readers of the novelists dealt with will find this manual a real assistance and a pleasure.

PHYLLIS BENTLEY

Who's Who in Jane Austen

A

ABBOTTS, THE TWO: Fellow-pupils of Harriet Smith at Miss Goddard's School. *Emma*

ABDY, OLD JOHN: A bedridden old man with rheumatic gout, for twenty-seven years clerk to the late Rev. Mr. Bates. *Emma*

ABDY, JOHN: Son of old John, ostler and head man at the Crown; well-to-do but cannot keep his father without help from the parish, about which he consults Mr. Elton. *Emma*

ALICE (LADY?): Eleanor Tilney asks Catherine Morland to write to her at Lord Longtown's home, under cover to Alice—possibly Lord Longtown's daughter, or possibly Eleanor's own maid. *Northanger Abbey*

ALICIA, LADY: She and Mrs. Frankland describe to Lady Russell certain windows in Pulteney Street as the best hung in Bath. She never gives dinners, not even to her own sister's family. *Persuasion*

ALLEN, MR.: A sensible, intelligent man, owns the chief of the property about Fullerton; when ordered to Bath to benefit his gouty constitution, he and his wife invite Catherine Morland to accompany them. Spends the Bath assemblies in the cardroom, will never wear a greatcoat, and gives Catherine more useful advice than his wife does. *Northanger Abbey*

ALLEN, MRS.: A good-humoured woman, fond of Catherine

3

Morland, acting as her chaperon when she takes her to Bath. She has neither beauty, genius, accomplishment or manner, only the air of a gentlewoman, a great deal of quiet, inactive good temper and a trifling turn of mind. Dress is her passion; she has 'a most harmless delight in being fine'. Her acquaintance with Mrs. Thorpe finds Catherine a friend in Isabella Thorpe. *Northanger Abbey*

ANDERSON, CHARLES: A friend of Tom Bertram, living in Baker Street, has a rather bold younger sister. *Mansfield Park*

ANDERSON, MISS: Younger sister of Charles Anderson, she embarrasses his friend Tom Bertram first by her gauche schoolgirl silence and later, when she has 'come out', by her unrecognisably bold familiarity. *Mansfield Park*

ANDREWS, MISS: A friend of Miss Thorpe, 'a sweet girl, one of the sweetest creatures in the world', who is netting herself 'the sweetest cloak you can conceive'; she looks as beautiful as an angel in her puce-coloured sarsenet (though there is something amazingly insipid about her), reads all the very horrid novels she can, but cannot get through the first volume of *Sir Charles Grandison*. *Northanger Abbey*

ANNESLEY, MRS.: Companion to Miss Darcy. A genteel, agreeable-looking woman, her tact and consideration show that she is more truly well-bred than Bingley's rich, haughty sisters. *Pride and Prejudice*

ATKINSON, MISS: A lady of Bath who has once dined with Mr. Elliot at the Wallises' and says he is the most agreeable man she ever was in company with. *Persuasion*

AYLMERS, THE: Pleasant people of lively agreeable manners and probably of morals and discretion to suit, living at Twickenham. Maria Rushworth stays with them at Easter and Henry Crawford her admirer has access there at all times. *Mansfield Park*

B

BADDELEY : Sir Thomas Bertram's butler. *Mansfield Park*

BALDWIN, ADMIRAL : A deplorable-looking personage, rough and rugged, all lines and wrinkles, whom Sir Walter Elliot guesses to be sixty though in fact he is forty—Sir Walter has never seen 'so wretched an example of what a sea-faring life can do'. *Persuasion*

BATES, MRS. : Widow of the Rev. Mr. Bates, former vicar of Highbury, a very old lady, almost past everything but tea and quadrille—fortunately, as she and her daughter now live in very cramped, impoverished circumstances. *Emma*

BATES, MISS HETTY : Daughter of the late Rev. Mr. Bates, though reduced from a social position of importance in his lifetime to increasing poverty, she enjoys 'a most uncommon degree of popularity for a woman neither young, handsome, rich nor married'. She has no intellectual resources to interest herself or others but she is a happy woman; it is 'her own universal good-will and contented temper which worked such wonders'. A great talker upon little matters, the flood of her conversation can bewilder and amaze, and is the subject of an unkind witticism that shows Emma's lack of humane sympathy. *Emma*

BATES, MISS JANE : *see* Fairfax, Mrs. Jane

BENNETT, MR. : Owner of Longbourne, which however is bequeathed away from his own daughters, as he has no son. An odd mixture of quick parts, sarcastic humour, reserve and caprice: marries his wife for her youth and beauty, and when disappointed in her mind and temper, he seeks consolation in books, country pursuits and ridiculing her ignorance and folly. His detached, satiric attitude is of no help in his five daughters' upbringing, for instead of useful correction he indulges in ironic comments on the younger girls' silliness. When the wildest and youngest, Lydia, runs away with Wickham and does not marry him, he is shocked into activity, though he soon relapses, and is unwilling to forgive her. Rates his sons-in-law according to their absurdity, and often goes to stay with his favourite daughter Elizabeth after her marriage, especially when least expected. *Pride and Prejudice*

BENNETT, MRS.: Née Gardiner. Daughter of a Meryton attorney, with a fortune of four thousand pounds, she attracts Mr. Bennett by her youth, beauty and appearance of good humour. In fact she is a woman of mean understanding, little information and uncertain temper, and her husband's sarcasm at her expense is lost on her. Her greatest anxiety is to marry her five daughters well, though her own vulgarity and improper upbringing of the younger girls is the chief obstacle to this ambition. *Pride and Prejudice*

BENNETT, ELIZABETH: Second daughter of the Bennetts, has lively playful manners, a light pleasing figure, and a face rendered uncommonly intelligent by the beautiful expression of her dark eyes. Forms a prejudice against the rich, proud Mr. Darcy, initially because he does not choose to dance with her, later believing he has unjustly impoverished Mr. Wickham, whose very handsome appearance and captivating manners predispose her in his favour. When she refuses to marry her father's cousin and heir, the foolish Mr. Collins, she is disappointed by the immediate acceptance he gains from her friend Charlotte Lucas. Charlotte's mercenary attitude contrasts with the delicacy of Elizabeth's favourite sister Jane, who is made unhappy by the departure of her admirer Mr. Bingley, persuaded by Mr. Darcy. Guessing this, Elizabeth is not pleased to meet Mr. Darcy again while he is staying with the Collinses, and is amazed and indignant when he proposes to her; she refuses angrily.

He writes to explain his conduct as regards Mr. Bingley and Mr. Wickham, whose profligacy he warns her of, and she comes to believe him, despise Wickham, and regret her prejudice. Travelling with her aunt and uncle in Derbyshire she meets him again by chance but their reconciliation is interrupted by the news of her younger sister Lydia's seduction by Wickham, and although Bingley is reunited with Jane it is not until she learns of Darcy's financial efforts to make Wickham marry Lydia that Elizabeth hopes for his continued affection. Lady Catherine de Bourgh's report of an interview with her encourages him, and they become engaged. Misled by her characteristic wit into prejudice—'I meant to be uncommonly clever in taking so decided a dislike to him, without any reason'— she adds to her wit and vivacity the solid advantages of his knowledge and judgment. *Pride and Prejudice*

BENNETT, JANE: Eldest daughter of the Bennetts, a very beautiful young woman of twenty-two whose good principles are united with remarkable kindness; she manages 'to take the good of everybody's character and make it still better, and say nothing of the bad'. In love for the first time with the rich Mr. Bingley, her sense of decorum prevents her showing her feelings, so that he is persuaded to break the acquaintance in view of her apparent indifference and unsuitable family and fortune. In spite of her even greater caution when he returns, realising his mistake, they are soon engaged, and their happiness seems assured, having 'for basis, the excellent understanding and super-excellent disposition of Jane, and a general similarity of feeling and taste between her and himself'. *Pride and Prejudice*

BENNETT, KITTY: The Bennetts' fourth daughter, not strong, has an irritating cough. She is a weaker character than her younger sister Lydia, by whom she is led, but being of more governable a temper, after Lydia's influence is removed she improves greatly. Thereafter she spends much time with her married elder sisters, becoming 'by proper attention and management less irritable, less ignorant and less insipid'. *Pride and Prejudice*

BENNETT, LYDIA: Youngest and favourite daughter of Mrs. Bennett. Boisterous, uncivil and good-humoured, her heedless behaviour, especially in flirting with the militia officers quartered in the village, harms her sisters' reputation; when she visits Brighton she is easily persuaded to run away with Wickham. Never taught to think seriously, she is unconcerned about marrying him, and when by Mr. Darcy's efforts she is found and a marriage brought about, she shows no shame: 'Lydia was Lydia still: untamed, unabashed, wild, noisy and fearless'. They live in Newcastle at first, later moving about, always in quest of cheaper lodgings, always spending more than they ought. However, she retains all the claims to reputation which her marriage gives her. *Pride and Prejudice*

BENNETT, MARY: The Bennetts' third daughter, who, being the least handsome, works hard for knowledge and accomplishments, and is always anxious to display them— with mortifying results for the family, for she has neither genius nor taste but a pedantic air and conceited manner. After three of her sisters marry, she has to accompany her mother into society and spend less time on her accomplishments. Moralises formally on everything from morning visits to her sister's seduction. *Pride and Prejudice*

BENWICK, CAPTAIN: An excellent young man, not tall, with a pleasing face and melancholy air. He is engaged to Fanny Harville but, just as he wins fortune and promotion, she dies. Grief overwhelms him, for he unites strong feelings with reflective and scholarly tastes. Apparently attracted to Anne Elliot, he later falls in love with Louisa Musgrove, while she is recovering from injuries at the Harvilles' home, and later still they become engaged. Though originally unlike, in his depression and her natural high spirits, his consolation and her illness bring them closer in character. His recovery from his bereavement is due to his 'affectionate heart. He must love somebody'. *Persuasion*

BERTRAM, EDMUND : Younger son of Sir Thomas, shows all the gentleness of an excellent nature even as a youth, when he comforts the child Fanny Price and without ostentation takes her part. He is to be a clergyman, a handicap in his courtship of Mary Crawford, a witty, worldly young woman who wants a fashionable life. He and Fanny Price object to the unsuitable, indiscreet theatricals at Mansfield Park, but he is won over by Mary's influence, and seems to have attracted her too, much to the distress of Fanny who has always loved him. However, when his married sister Maria elopes with Mary's brother, her callous, irreligious attitude to their adultery disillusions him. After a due period of inconsolable depression he marries Fanny. Upright, sensible and tactful, he wins Mary against her will by the charm of sincerity, steadiness and integrity. *Mansfield Park*

BERTRAM, JULIA : Younger daughter of Sir Thomas, fair and handsome. She is attracted to Henry Crawford and bitterly jealous when he flirts instead with her engaged sister Maria. She overcomes her feelings when he leaves, and accompanies her sister on her wedding tour and later to London. Here she allows the attentions of Mr. Yates, though probably she only accepts and elopes with him to escape her father's wrath and increased severity after Maria's elopement. After her marriage she is humble and wishes to be forgiven. She is more fortunate than Maria in spite of a similarly superficial education, partly because she is less spoilt by her aunt Norris and partly because her temper is naturally the easiest of the two and her feelings, though quick, are more easily controlled. *Mansfield Park*

BERTRAM, MARIA: Elder daughter of Sir Thomas, handsome, tall and fair: her expensive education has not instilled true principles, an omission aggravated by the indulgence and flattery of her aunt Norris, and her father's corrective severity only makes her conceal her feelings. She becomes engaged to the foolish but rich owner of Sotherton Grange, Mr. Rushworth, without loving or respecting him, then marries him, out of pride, when hopes raised by Henry Crawford's flirtation with her are disappointed. After marriage, her headstrong spirit and wild passions are revealed when she elopes with the almost reluctant Crawford, refusing to leave him until convinced that he will not marry her. She is then relegated by her father to a remote house with her doting, nagging aunt, where their tempers probably become their punishment. *Mansfield Park*

BERTRAM, SIR THOMAS: Baronet and Member of Parliament, marries Miss Maria Ward. A grave, stately, oratorical man, father of Tom, Edmund, Maria and Julia. He agrees to bring up his wife's niece Fanny Price but recommends that she remembers her different expectations, a difference that reinforces his daughters in their pride and self-esteem. Trying to counteract the flattery of the girls' aunt Norris he only loses their confidence. Allows Maria to marry the rich, stupid Mr. Rushworth, evidently without loving him, but finds her feelings are not as weak as he thinks when she elopes and lives in adultery with Henry Crawford: 'with all the cost and care of an anxious and expensive education he had brought up his daughters without their understanding their first duties or his being acquainted with their character and temper'. In the event his niece Fanny, thanks to her education in humility and unworldliness, turns out more the daughter he wants and is welcomed as the wife of his younger son Edmund. *Mansfield Park*

BERTRAM, LADY (MARIA): Née Ward. Marries Sir

Thomas as a handsome girl with only seven thousand pounds (three thousand short of his market value). A woman of very tranquil feelings and a temper remarkably easy and indolent, and though she does not think deeply she thinks justly, guided by Sir Thomas on all important points (and most unimportant points too). She benefits by the partial adoption of her sister's daughter Fanny Price, who grows up to be a companion and assistant to her. She relies on Fanny much more than on her own selfish daughters even before they disgrace the family by their elopements. To their unsteady morals her own indolence no doubt contributes, but she never considers excusing or making light of their conduct. Comes to love Fanny's sister and successor Susan even more. *Mansfield Park*

BERTRAM, TOM: Eldest son of Sir Thomas Bertram, a wild, extravagant youth, so that the church living (with its income) destined for his younger brother has instead to be sold to pay his debts. Just entering life, full of spirits and feeling himself born only for expense and enjoyment, he is thoughtlessly selfish. He arranges for his family and friends to act a play during his father's absence abroad, which hurts Sir Thomas's feelings, the play and the atmosphere being unsuitable and encouraging everyone to be as selfish as himself. After a fall and neglected cold he becomes dangerously ill: in his suffering he learns to think—both suffering and thought are new experiences for him. Thereafter he becomes what he ought to be—useful to his father, steady and quiet, and no longer living merely for himself. *Mansfield Park*

BETTY: Mrs. Jennings' maid, who returns to London by public coach to leave room for the Miss Dashwoods in her mistress's carriage. Has a sister looking for a place as housemaid. *Sense and Sensibility*

BICKERTON, MISS: A parlour boarder at Miss Goddard's

school, with whom Harriet Smith is walking when they are accosted by gypsies. Terrified, she runs away, leaving Harriet alone. *Emma*

BINGLEY, MISS CAROLINE : The younger of Mr. Bingley's two sisters, a very fine lady not deficient in good humour and conversation when pleased, but proud and conceited. Accompanying her brother to Netherfield, she forms a friendship with Jane Bennett, but seeing her brother's attraction to her and considering her family and fortune too low, she contrives to separate them. Her further contrivances to captivate Mr. Darcy are less successful; she is jealous of his preference for Elizabeth Bennett, though when all her plans are foiled, and he marries Elizabeth, she pays off all arrears of civility in order to remain on visiting terms. *Pride and Prejudice*

BINGLEY, MR. CHARLES : A good-looking and gentleman-like young man of twenty-three, of a respectable family in the north of England, whose fortune of a hundred thousand pounds was made in trade. The easiness, openness and ductility of his temper are matched by his impulsiveness; on impulse he rents the Netherfield estate, where he meets and falls in love with Jane Bennett. However, his sisters and friend Mr. Darcy consider her family and fortune too low, and are able to persuade him, thanks to his modesty, to believe she does not care for him. Later Darcy learns from Jane's sister that she really loves him, confesses the mistake, and they are reunited and soon married. His pleasant, generous, tolerant nature makes him charming, but in, for instance, his dependence on Darcy's opinion, he shows some lack of firmness and judgment. *Pride and Prejudice*

BIRD, MRS. : Née Millman, an old acquaintance of Mrs. Elton's, instanced as an example of a musical young lady who gives up music after marriage. *Emma*

BOURGH, MISS ANNE DE : Lady Catherine's only child,

heiress of Rosings, a small, thin girl whose health is too poor for her to attempt any accomplishments: looks sickly and cross. *Pride and Prejudice*

BOURGH, SIR LEWIS DE: Late husband of Lady Catherine. *Pride and Prejudice*

BOURGH, LADY CATHERINE DE: A tall, large woman with strongly marked features and an authoritative manner. Aunt of Mr. Darcy and patroness of the Bennetts' cousin, she rules her family, household and neighbourhood, settles their differences, silences their complaints, and scolds them into harmony and plenty. Having planned a match between her daughter and her nephew, she is alarmed by reports of his attentions to Elizabeth Bennett, whose family she considers a contamination for the Darcys, but after she impertinently demands that Elizabeth renounce him, her report of her failure encourages him to propose. On their marriage she writes an angry and abusive letter, but later is reconciled. Her pride is a ridiculous exaggeration of Darcy's. *Pride and Prejudice*

BRAGGE, MR.: A neighbour of Mr. Suckling, once went to London with him twice in one week with four horses. *Emma*

BRAGGE, MRS.: A cousin of Mr. Suckling, who moves in the first circles and allows wax candles in her schoolroom, which makes her a sought-after employer of governesses. *Emma*

BRAND, ADMIRAL: Acquaintance of Admiral Croft, a shabby fellow who plays him a pitiful trick, taking away some of his best men. Also his BROTHER. *Persuasion*

BRANDON, COLONEL: Owner of Delaford, a good estate in Dorset, which he inherits too late after his cousin and sweetheart Eliza has been married to his elder brother. Going abroad to avoid temptation, he returns to find that after ill-treatment has forced her to elope, she has been divorced and, sunk in misery, is dying in a debtors' prison. Takes charge of her illegitimate daughter Eliza, and when she in turn is seduced by Willoughby, rescues her and fights a duel with him. Falls in love with 17-year-old Marianne Dashwood who considers him at thirty-five to be a dull, elderly man; suffers to see her apparently engaged to Willoughby, and when she is jilted is able to confirm her lucky escape by telling Eliza's history. Kindly gives a church living to the disinherited Edward Ferrars, and later marries Marianne, who learns to love him wholeheartedly in spite of his incipient rheumatism and flannel waistcoat. Has a sister in Avignon. *Sense and Sensibility*

BRANDON, MR.: Brother of Colonel Brandon, whose childhood sweetheart, their rich cousin Eliza, he marries, to restore the family fortunes, without loving or deserving her. His pleasures are not what they ought to be, and his unkind treatment drives her to elope, whereupon he divorces her. He dies and Colonel Brandon inherits the estate five years before he meets the Dashwoods. *Sense and Sensibility*

BRANDON, MRS. ELIZA: Colonel Brandon's cousin and childhood sweetheart, an heiress who is persuaded against her will to marry his elder brother, who ill-treats her. She runs away, is divorced, changes lovers, and is dying of consumption in a debtors' prison when the Colonel returns to England and traces her. Has one illegitimate daughter, Eliza Williams. *Sense and Sensibility*

BRIGDEN, CAPTAIN: A friend of Admiral Croft, he stares to see anyone with the Admiral but his wife. *Persuasion*

BROWN, MRS.: Gives a party in Bath at which Mr. Elton and Miss Hawkins further their acquaintance. *Emma*

BROWN, MRS.: Appears at the Commissioner's in Gibraltar with hair arranged in the current English fashion, which makes the unprepared William Price think she is mad. *Mansfield Park*

BURGESS, MRS.: Miss Steele goes off to stay with her in Exeter after being left penniless when her sister elopes. *Sense and Sensibility*

C

CAMPBELL, COLONEL: A friend of Jane Fairfax's father, who regards him highly and is grateful for his nursing during camp fever. After his death he takes notice of his little daughter Jane and eventually takes her into his home as a companion for his own daughter (*see* Dixon, Mrs.). By giving her an education he hopes to provide her with the means of earning her living as a governess. Also CAMPBELL, MRS.: his wife. Both find it hard to part with Jane when she grows up. *Emma*

CAMPBELL, MR.: The surgeon of the *Thrush* where William Price is second lieutenant, accompanies his friend William on board. *Mansfield Park*

CAREYS, THE: Two Miss Careys come over to Barton from Newton for the proposed trip to Whitewell, and when that is cancelled they stay to dinner with the Middletons, joined by some more of the Careys. *Sense and Sensibility*

CARTER, CAPTAIN: An officer of the militia regiment quartered at Meryton, admired by Lydia Bennett. *Pride and Prejudice*

CARTERET, THE HONOURABLE MISS: A young lady of no distinction, with little to say for herself, and so plain and so awkward that only her birth, as daughter of Viscountess Dalrymple, makes her acceptable to the Elliots. *Persuasion*

CARTWRIGHT: Mrs. Jennings has to 'settle with' him or her on returning to London. *Sense and Sensibility*

CHAMBERLAYNE: One of the officers in the militia quartered at Meryton. Lydia Bennett's idea of a good joke is to dress him as a woman in her Aunt Phillip's gown. *Pride and Prejudice*

CHAPMAN, MRS.: Lady's maid to Lady Bertram, who spontaneously and unprompted thinks of sending her to dress Fanny for her first ball, too late of course to be of any use. *Mansfield Park*

CHARLES, SIR: A friend of Admiral Crawford, he has some influence with the First Lord of the Admiralty. By his offices William Price is made Lieutenant. *Mansfield Park*

CHARLES: A postilion; rides one of the leaders of Lady Bertram's coach. *Mansfield Park*

CHURCHILL, MR.: Owner of Enscombe, of a great Yorkshire family, brother of Mr. Weston's first wife, who is angry at the match and ceremoniously casts her off, though some reconciliation during her last illness leads to the adoption of her son Frank. Ruled by his dominating, ill-tempered wife, he is an easy, guidable man, and when she dies he speedily accepts Frank's engagement to Jane Fairfax; they marry and go to live with him on the best of terms. *Emma*

CHURCHILL, MRS.: Sister-in-law of Mr. Weston's first wife, proud, self-important woman, though barely a gentleman's daughter before her marriage. Her own lack of children leads to their adoption of young Frank, and she is very fond of him, possessively curtailing his visits elsewhere, even to his own father. Her pleas of ill-health are assumed to be pretence, until she dies unexpectedly and, 'After being disliked for at least twenty-five years, was now spoken of with compassionate allowances'. Her uncertain temper is the reason for Frank's engagement being secret, but her influence disappears with her death. *Emma*

CHURCHILL, FRANK: Son of Mr. Weston and his first wife, is brought up from infancy by his rich maternal uncle and aunt, the Churchills of Enscombe. Tacitly supposed to be their heir, he takes their name at twenty-one. Sees his affectionate father once a year in London, and never is allowed by his possessive aunt to visit his native Highbury until he is twenty-three. A very handsome young man with his father's spirit and liveliness, he is soon a favourite and Emma Woodhouse is temporarily attracted to him. He rescues Harriet Smith from gypsies, which seems favourable to romance, but in fact his visits are due to his secret engagement to Jane Fairfax, now staying with her Highbury relatives. He successfully disguises their relationship but she, distressed, breaks it off: however, the death of his jealous aunt enables them to marry. Less straightforward than his name implies, he comes to Highbury under false pretences, though he excuses his seeming flirtation with Emma by assuming she guesses the truth; like her, he is 'Always deceived in fact by his own wishes' and is 'too much indebted to the event for his acquittal'. *Emma*

CLARKE, MRS.: An intimate acquaintance of Mrs. Jennings, meets her in Kensington Gardens. *Sense and Sensibility*

CLAY, MRS. PENELOPE: Daughter of Mr. Shepherd, returns to her father's house, a widow after an unprosperous marriage, with two children. A clever young woman who understands the art of pleasing, she becomes Elizabeth Elliot's intimate friend and has designs of marrying Sir Walter Elliot. In spite of her freckles, projecting tooth and clumsy wrist, she is altogether well-looking and thinks her flattery is likely to succeed, until Sir Walter's heir Mr. Elliot, opposed to a marriage that might disinherit him, foils her by gaining her affections and takes her away as his mistress. 'She has abilities, however, as well as affections,' and after preventing her from being the wife of Sir Walter he may 'be wheedled and caressed into making her the wife of Sir William'. *Persuasion*

COLE, MR.: A friendly, liberal, unpretending man, only moderately genteel, his origins being in trade. In later years he prospers very much and expands his style of living until almost equal to Mr. Woodhouse's at Hartfield. Fond of company, he cannot touch malt liquor, being very bilious. *Emma*

COLE, MRS.: A good-natured woman, a steady friend to the Bates'. Has little girls. *Emma*

COLLINS, MR.: A cousin of the Bennetts, who is to inherit their family estate, as Mr. Bennett has no son. He is a tall, heavy-looking young man of five and twenty; his air is grave and stately, his manners very formal. Not a sensible man, he has been brought up by an illiterate miserly father, then, on becoming a clergyman, is patronised by Lady Catherine de Bourgh, whom he venerates; he is 'altogether a mixture of pride and obsequiousness, self-importance and humility'. Wishes to compensate the Bennetts for inheriting their estate by marrying one of the sisters, but being refused by Elizabeth, proposes to her friend Charlotte Lucas, who manages him so well that he marvels at their unanimity, concluding 'We seem to have been designed for each other'. *Pride and Prejudice*

COOPER, MRS. JAMES: Née Millman. Instanced as an example of a musical young lady who gives up music after marriage. *Emma*

COURTENEY, GENERAL: General Tilney is disappointed in hopes of seeing him in Bath. *Northanger Abbey*

COURTLAND, LORD: A friend of Robert Ferrars who asks

his advice on three cottage designs—all three of which Robert throws on the fire. *Sense and Sensibility*

COX, MR.: The lawyer of Highbury. *Emma*

COX, ANNE: Daughter of the Highbury lawyer; she and her sister are considered by Emma Woodhouse to be 'without exception the most vulgar girls in Highbury'. Also COX, MISS: her sister. *Emma*

COX, WILLIAM: Son of Mr. Cox, also a lawyer, fleetingly considered by Emma as a match for Harriet Smith. There is also a second YOUNG COX. *Emma*

CRAWFORD, ADMIRAL: Uncle of Henry and Mary Crawford, whom he brings up when they are orphaned. A man of vicious conduct, he disagrees with his wife in everything and, after her death, brings his mistress to live under his roof so that Mary has to leave. He is persuaded by his favourite, Henry, to use his influence to have William Price made a lieutenant. *Mansfield Park*

CRAWFORD, MRS.: Wife of Admiral Crawford, ill-treated by him; her favourite niece, Mary, dislikes the Admiral for her sake. *Mansfield Park*

CRAWFORD, HENRY: Brother of Mary Crawford, comes with her to visit his half-sister Mrs. Grant at the Mansfield Parsonage. Though not handsome, he has air and countenance, lively pleasant manners and a good estate in Norfolk, but having been brought up by his dissolute uncle, the Admiral, his principles are unsound. Flirts with Maria Bertram under her fiancé's nose, during the Mansfield Park amateur theatricals, in which he is the best actor. On a second visit he plans to make shy Fanny Price love him, but falls in love with her himself. He tries to win her by obtaining promotion for her favourite sailor brother, but she, already in love with her cousin Edmund, refuses him. While she is away visiting her parents he meets Maria again, now married, is annoyed by her resentful coldness, succeeds in attracting her again, and finds himself eloping with her because he cannot help it. He will not marry Maria after her divorce, and they part. Ruined by early indulgence and bad domestic example, he indulges the freaks of cold-blooded vanity a little too long, and being also a man of sense, his value for what he loses brings its punishment of self-reproach and regret. *Mansfield Park*

CRAWFORD, MARY: Sister of Henry, half-sister of Mrs. Grant, whom she visits at Mansfield Parsonage. A very pretty, dark, witty girl with twenty thousand pounds. Though ambitious she falls in love with Edmund Bertram in spite of his small fortune and vocation for the Church. Her charms are powerful enough to tempt him to join the amateur theatricals against his better judgment, but upon her brother's seduction of Mrs. Rushworth, her casual comments reveal unsound principles and shock Edmund— 'No reluctance, no horror, no feminine—shall I say? no modest loathings'. She loses her power over him, but the charm of his sincerity, steadiness and integrity make her dissatisfied thereafter with her more frivolous suitors. Lives for some years with her sister, whose kindness and tranquillity she needs. Kind and generous, her lack of principle means she is likely to be kind in the wrong place as well as the right. *Mansfield Park*

CROFT, ADMIRAL: A native of Somerset, a Rear Admiral of the White, takes part in the Trafalgar action, then is stationed in the East Indies. Coming on shore, he rents Kellynch Hall from Sir Walter Elliot. His manners are unceremonious, frank and pleasing, although devoid of tact and correctness. *Persuasion*

CROFT, MRS.: Wife of Admiral Croft, sister of Captain Wentworth. Neither tall nor fat, she has a squareness, uprightness and vigour of form which gives importance to her person and her weatherbeaten complexion makes her look older than her thirty-eight years. Her open, decided manners and good humour are like her brother's; she is an excellent example of a sailor's wife: when the admiral is ordered to exercise, 'Mrs. Croft seemed to go shares with him in everything and to walk for her life to do him good'. *Persuasion*

D

DALRYMPLE, THE LATE VISCOUNT: Has once been in company with his relation Sir Walter Elliot. His death is not greeted with a letter of condolence from the Elliots, an omission that causes offence and a breach between the families. *Persuasion*

DALRYMPLE, THE DOWAGER VISCOUNTESS: Cousin of the Elliots, though relations have been broken between them for some time. When she visits Bath while the Elliots are there, her acquaintance is sought and boasted of— causelessly, as she is reputed 'a charming woman' only for her smiles and civil answers, without any superiority of manner, accomplishment or understanding. Also her daughter: *see* CARTERET, MISS. *Persuasion*

DARCY, THE LATE MR.: Father of Fitzwilliam Darcy, makes a favourite of his steward's son, the undeserving George Wickham. *Pride and Prejudice*

DARCY, LADY ANNE: Mother of Mr. Darcy, she and her sister Lady Catherine de Bourgh plan a match between her son and Miss Anne de Bourgh while they are children. *Pride and Prejudice*

DARCY, MR. FITZWILLIAM: A very rich man of twenty-eight with a fine tall person, handsome features and noble mien, but haughty, reserved and fastidious. A close friend of Mr. Bingley, though superior to him in understanding and of an opposite temperament, he discourages his attachment to Jane Bennett, believing her not only unsuitable in family and fortune, but also indifferent. His pride, which prevents him explaining his motives and feelings, leads to a general dislike of him, and belief that he has wronged and impoverished the pleasant affable Mr. Wickham. His pride however is partly overcome by his attraction to Jane's sister Elizabeth, and he is shocked when she refuses to marry him. He explains by letter his motives with regard to Bingley and Wickham, who as well as other injuries has tried to elope with his sister Miss Darcy. Meeting Elizabeth again by chance he wishes to prove he is less haughty and uncivil than she thinks, and shows her particular courtesy. When her youngest sister Lydia elopes with Wickham, for Elizabeth's sake he finds and bribes him to marry Lydia. Later he also undoes his injuries of Jane by reuniting her with Bingley, but it is the report by his aunt Lady Catherine de Bourgh that Elizabeth will not promise to renounce him that encourages him to propose again, and this time he is accepted. As Mary Bennett says, 'Pride relates more to our opinion of ourselves' and Darcy's indifference to others' opinions leads to the misunderstandings about Wickham and his impolitely condescending proposal to Elizabeth. Their marriage is likely to be happy, for by her ease and liveliness his mind should be softened and his manners improved. *Pride and Prejudice*

DARCY, MISS GEORGIANA: Mr. Darcy's sister. After she leaves school, she lives with Mrs. Younge in London, but while visiting Ramsgate at fifteen is persuaded by Wickham to elope with him, partly for revenge on the family, partly for her fortune of thirty thousand pounds, However, she is led by her affection for her brother to confess the plan to him. Tall, womanly and graceful, she is less handsome than her brother, but appears sensible and good humoured. Her reputation for extreme pride arises only from her extreme shyness. *Pride and Prejudice*

DAWSON: A servant of Lady Catherine de Bourgh, probably her lady's maid, who 'does not object' to travelling on the barouche box to make room inside the barouche for guests. *Pride and Prejudice*

DASHWOOD, MR.: Owner of Norland Park and its large estate, a single man of an old family who lives to a very advanced age. After his sister's death he invites the family of his nephew and heir Henry Dashwood to live with him, gains comfort and cheerfulness from their society, but bequeathes the estate to Henry so secured that it must pass to Henry's son, already rich, not to his poorly endowed wife and daughters. *Sense and Sensibility*

DASHWOOD, MISS: Old Mr. Dashwood's sister, for many years his housekeeper and companion, dies ten years before him. *Sense and Sensibility*

DASHWOOD, ELINOR: Eldest daughter of Henry and Mrs. Dashwood, pretty and with great strength of understanding and coolness of judgment. She has an excellent heart, her disposition is affectionate and her feelings are strong but she knows how to govern them, and her sense is constantly necessary to check the unrestrained sensibility of her mother and sister Marianne. In love with her brother's relative Edward Ferrars, who seems also attached to her, she is slighted by his family, who have greater ambitions for him; her mother indignantly moves from their brother's home to a cottage in Devonshire. Later the vulgar, ambitious Lucy Steele reveals the cause of Edward's reticence by confiding that he is secretly engaged to her. Elinor controls her feelings without betraying them, and wishes that Marianne would show equal restraint in her attachment to Willoughby. On a visit to the vulgar Mrs. Jennings in London, accepted from Marianne's determination at all costs to see Willoughby again, it is Elinor who has to pay polite attention to their hostess and who later has to console and tend Marianne's unrestrained grief when jilted. Edward's mother discovers his engagement and disinherits him, and Elinor is asked to offer him Colonel Brandon's gift of a church living that will enable him to marry her rival. Fulfilling all these tasks with fortitude, she is rewarded, after false news of Edward's marriage, by finding him free (Lucy having eloped with his brother) and anxious to marry her. They live in great content at Delaford Rectory. The only member of her family to behave with dignity and self-control, she is given to rather righteous reproofs of others' conduct. *Sense and Sensibility*

DASHWOOD, HARRY: Only son of John and Fanny Dashwood, whose attractions (by no means unusual in a child of two or three years old)—cunning tricks and a great deal of noise—outweighs with old Mr. Dashwood the constant affection of his nieces; Harry has the estate bequeathed to him in preference to them. *Sense and Sensibility*

DASHWOOD, HENRY: Nephew of the late owner of Norland Park, inherits it conditionally, secured to his son's family, though it is more needed by his wife and daughters. Hopeful of saving enough from the estate to leave them comfortable, he in fact dies only a year after his uncle, after begging his son to assist them. *Sense and Sensibility*

DASHWOOD, MRS.: Second wife of Henry Dashwood, mother of Elinor, Marianne and Margaret, a generous, impulsive, romantic woman of forty. Without selfishness or folly, she has an eagerness of mind that might often lead her into imprudence but for Elinor's good advice. Very like Marianne in character, she encourages her in unworldly romance. They indulge each other's hopes and griefs with no thought of rational restraint. After her husband's death, sensitive and tactful herself, she is affronted by her daughter-in-law's rudeness, and leaves her former home to live in a cottage in Barton, Devonshire. She is unreservedly won over by the handsome Willoughby, and being too delicate to ask the confidence of him or Marianne, she imposes no caution on their relationship, so that later, when Willoughby denies serious intentions, Marianne is heartbroken. Afterwards promotes her marriage with Colonel Brandon. A charming and affectionate mother, 'a man could not very well be in love with either of her daughters, without extending the passion to her'. *Sense and Sensibility*

DASHWOOD, JOHN: Son of Henry Dashwood by his first marriage, half-brother to Elinor, Marianne and Margaret. He has not the strong feelings of the rest of the family, but is 'not an ill-disposed young man, unless to be cold hearted and rather selfish is to be ill-disposed', and might have improved further if he had married a more amiable woman than his narrow-minded wife. Entreated by his dying father to assist his half-sisters, he decides he need only help them in a neighbourly way, thereafter feeling rather guilty about his lack of generosity. *Sense and Sensibility*

DASHWOOD, MRS. JOHN (FANNY): Née Ferrars. Wife of John Dashwood and a strong caricature of himself—more narrow-minded and selfish. When her brother Edward Ferrars seems attracted to her sister-in-law Elinor, she takes care to hint this is not acceptable to their family ambitions, and goes into hysterics when his secret engagement to Lucy Steele is revealed. Like the socially successful Lady Middleton, she has an insipid propriety of demeanor and a general want of understanding. Her husband dotes on her. *Sense and Sensibility*

DASHWOOD, MARGARET: Youngest of the Dashwood

sisters, a good-humoured, well-disposed girl, who has imbibed a good deal of Marianne's romance without having much of her sense, and does not at thirteen bid fair to equal her sisters. Embarrasses them at times by her indiscretion, and has reached an age highly suitable for dancing by the time Marianne marries. *Sense and Sensibility*

DASHWOOD, MARIANNE: Second daughter of Mrs. Dashwood, a beautiful girl of seventeen with clear brown skin, good features and very dark eyes. She is sensible and clever but eager in everything, 'her sorrows, her joys could have no moderation'. Despising reserve and prudence she shows her love for the equally ardent Willoughby without asking any assurances on his part, so that when he jilts her she is both deeply wounded and exposed to the comments of society. She always indulges her feelings and makes no effort to overcome her grief. Even when her sister Elinor explains that she too has been disappointed but has struggled to regain calm, she reproaches herself but feels too weak to follow her example. Only after her self-indulgent rambles in the wet, cold countryside have resulted in a dangerous fever does she resolve to act with more consideration for her family. She lives to overcome her feelings and, against all previous resolutions, marries the older Colonel Brandon with no feelings stronger than esteem and lively friendship: but she cannot love by halves and soon becomes devoted to him. *Sense and Sensibility*

DAVIES, DOCTOR: A doctor of divinity, about whose (probably imaginary) intentions Miss Steele likes to be teased. His favourite colour is pink. *Sense and Sensibility*

DAVIS, CHARLOTTE: Having raised then disappointed Isabella Thorpe's expectations, Captain Tilney spends his last two days in Bath at Charlotte Davis' side. *Northanger Abbey*

DENNISON, MRS.: An acquaintance of Mrs. John

Dashwood, she embarrasses her by assuming the Miss Dashwoods are staying with her (as they ought to be) and sends a collective invitation to her musical party. *Sense and Sensibility*

DENNY, MR.: An officer in the militia quartered at Meryton, a chance acquaintance of Mr. Wickham whom he persuades to join the regiment. Later refuses to admit any knowledge of Wickham's elopement. *Pride and Prejudice*

DIXON, MR.: A young man, rich and agreeable, owner of Balycraig in Ireland. Marries Colonel Campbell's daughter. Saves Jane Fairfax from being swept overboard at Weymouth; Emma Woodhouse wrongly fancies he is secretly in love with Jane. *Emma*

DIXON, MRS.: Daughter of Mr. and Mrs. Campbell, she becomes so attached to Jane Fairfax that they are brought up together. Although absolutely plain, but extremely elegant and amiable, she shows no jealousy of her friend's beauty, and in fact is preferred and married by Mr. Dixon. *Emma*

DONAVAN, MR.: A doctor or apothecary who, while reassuring Mrs. Palmer that her baby only has 'the red gum', tells her and Mrs. Jennings of the uproar at Mrs. John Dashwood's house, where she has discovered her brother Edward's secret engagement to her guest Lucy Steele. He prepares to be called also to Edward's mother, who is bound to need his attentions too when she hears the news. *Sense and Sensibility*

DOROTHY: The imaginary housekeeper, old, bent and sinister, an epitome of the ancient, mysterious retainers of Gothic horror novels. Henry Tilney pretends she will await his guest, Catherine Morland, at Northanger Abbey. *Northanger Abbey*

DREW, SIR ARCHIBALD: Meets his acquaintance, Admiral

Croft, and Anne Elliot in the street, and greets her in mistake for Mrs Croft. An old man who regrets the peace. Also his GRANDSON. *Persuasion*

DUKE, THE: Attends Lord Ravenshaw's houseparty, and takes the role of Frederick in their interrupted amateur production of *Lovers' Vows*. He is thought very great by many. *Mansfield Park*

DURANDS, THE LITTLE: Well-known Bath figures, described by Mrs. Smith: they attend concerts 'with their mouths open to catch the music; like unfledged sparrows ready to be fed'. *Persuasion*

E

ELLIOT, SIR——: A friend of Robert Ferrars, living in a cottage near Dartford. *Sense and Sensibility*

ELLIOT, LADY: Wishes to give a dance in her 'cottage' but fears there will not be enough room, a difficulty solved by her guest Robert Ferrars. *Sense and Sensibility*

ELLIOT, ANNE: Second daughter of Sir Walter. With exceptional elegance of mind and sweetness of character, Anne has been a very pretty girl but at twenty-seven has lost her bloom. Becoming engaged to Captain Wentworth at nineteen, she is discouraged by her father's pride and coldness and more vigorously persuaded by her godmother and friend Lady Russell to give him up, which she does partly for his own sake, though still in love with him. She later refuses Charles Musgrove for that reason. She stays with her younger sister, while her father and elder sister move to Bath to economise, letting their home to the Crofts, who are the brother-in-law and sister of Captain Wentworth who visits them there. He is still unmarried and resentful towards Anne for her lack of firmness. However, her rational competence wins his respect again when Louisa Musgrove, whom he admires, confuses firmness with obstinacy and precipitates an accident in which she is injured. When she rejoins her family in Bath she finds she has two admirers, her cousin Mr. Elliot and Captain Wentworth. As her taste is for the open frankness of Wentworth and his sailor friends, she is suspicious of Elliot's calculated reserve, and her friendship with Mrs. Smith, a widowed invalid and former schoolfriend who knows him, leads to revelations of his past bad conduct and present cunning designs. Arriving at an understanding with Captain Wentworth, she marries him: 'She had been forced into prudence in her youth, she learned romance as she grew older—the natural sequel of an unnatural beginning.' *Persuasion*

ELLIOT, ELIZABETH: Eldest daughter of Sir Walter, a proud, unfeeling woman, unmarried, who is handsomer at twenty-nine than she was ten years before, though she would rejoice to be certain of being properly solicited by baronet-blood within the next twelvemonth or so. She has always intended to marry her father's nephew and heir William Elliot, who instead speaks slightingly of the family and marries a rich vulgar woman. Annoyed, she is reconciled to him when his wife dies and he seems to be attracted to her. She makes a confidante of the plain, clever widow Mrs. Clay, and when the Elliots go to live more economically in Bath, takes her in preference to her own sister Anne, not seeing her designs on Sir Walter. She is shocked and mortified when Mr. Elliot elopes with Mrs. Clay, and thereafter is unsought by any other suitor. As haughty as her father and less civil, she is contemptuous of her inferiors and deferential to her superiors in rank. *Persuasion*

ELLIOT, MARY: *see* MUSGROVE, MARY

ELLIOT, SIR WALTER: Of Kellynch Hall, father of Elizabeth, Anne and Mary, 'a man who, for his own amusement, never took up any book but the Baronetage' —vanity is the beginning and end of his character. His pride in his rank leads him to disparage commoners and flatter superiors, and his pride in his handsome appearance equally makes him despise unattractive acquaintances. His good looks and rank however probably won him his excellent wife, after whose death ('having met with one or two private disappointments in very unreasonable applications') he remains single, though, being susceptible to flattery, is in danger from the plain but clever Mrs. Clay. An extravagant, neglectful landowner, he runs into debt and has to let Kellynch Hall and live economically in Bath. Though he has discouraged Anne's engagement to Captain Wentworth, eight years later when it is renewed it seems Wentworth is 'quite worthy to address the daughter of a foolish spendthrift baronet who had not had principle or sense enough to maintain himself in the situation in which Providence had placed him'. *Persuasion*

ELLIOT, LADY: Wife of Sir Walter, of very superior character to anything deserved by his own. An excellent woman, sensible and amiable, she humours and softens or conceals his failings and promotes his real respectability for seventeen years: it is after her death that he gets into debt. *Persuasion*

ELLIOT, THE SECOND SIR WALTER: Grandfather of Mr. William Elliot, the present Sir Walter's heir. *Persuasion*

ELLIOT, WILLIAM WALTER: Nephew and presumed heir of Sir Walter Elliot. As a young man he despises the baronet and rejects the possibility of marrying his eldest daughter Elizabeth, preferring the independence of marrying a rich but plebian woman. Growing older he comes to value rank more, and when his wife dies and he hears that the clever widow Mrs. Clay has designs on Sir Walter, he plans to keep him unmarried by marrying into the family himself, first approaching Elizabeth, later becoming attracted to her younger sister Anne. She learns from her friend Mrs. Smith, whose husband was led to ruin by Mr. Elliot, that he is not as pleasant as he seems; ungrateful and unwilling to trouble himself for others, he refuses to act as executor of her husband's will to help Mrs. Smith in her extreme poverty. Disappointed by Anne's engagement to Wentworth, he leaves Bath and proves to have foiled Mrs. Clay by winning her affections, as she goes with him: he may yet end by marrying her. Though he is agreeable and intelligent, with good understanding, correct opinions and knowledge of the world, there is 'never any burst of feeling, any warmth of imagination or delight'; no genuine feeling supports his good manners. *Persuasion*

ELLIOT, MRS. : Daughter of a grazier, granddaughter of a butcher, but very rich, a fine woman with a decent education, falls in love with William Elliot, who marries her for her money. Dies after not a very happy marriage. *Persuasion*

ELLIS : A maid of the Bertrams, waits on Maria and Julia. *Mansfield Park*

ELLISONS, THE : Guardians of Sophia Grey, the heiress Willoughby marries. They are glad to have her married because she and Mrs. Ellison never agree. *Sense and Sensibility*

ELTON, MR. PHILIP : Vicar of Highbury, a young man of six or seven and twenty, considered good-looking with effusive manners and a broad handsome face, though with a certain want of elegance of feature: assumed by Emma Woodhouse to be courting the penniless, illegitimate but beautiful Harriet Smith, he in fact sets a higher value on himself and has designs on Emma herself, and is resentful at her refusal. Soon afterwards he marries the showy, inelegant Augusta Hawkins who exactly suits him, but they both harbour a grudge against Emma. *Emma*

ELTON, MRS.: Née Hawkins, meets the vicar Mr. Elton at Bath where he is recovering from his refusal by Emma Woodhouse, and marries him. She has as many thousand pounds as will always be called ten, all her distinction lying in her elder sister Selina being very well married to a gentleman who keeps two carriages. A vain woman, extremely well satisfied with herself, with manners formed in a bad school, pert and familiar, she has Emma's weakness for managing other people but with no tact or moderation. Patronises Jane Fairfax, for whom she finds a place as governess against Jane's will. *Emma*

EMILY and SOPHIA: Two of the sweetest girls in the world, walking with Anne Thorpe, who have been her dear friends all the morning. Though rejected as a companion by her brother because of her thick ankles, at least Anne has the friendship of an Emily and a Sophia to console her. *Northanger Abbey*

F

FAIRFAX, LIEUTENANT: An infantry officer, marries Jane Bates, daughter of the former vicar of Highbury. He is killed in action abroad, his wife dying soon afterwards. He is remembered by his friend Colonel Campbell as an excellent officer and most deserving young man, particularly for saving the Colonel's life by nursing him through camp fever. *Emma*

FAIRFAX, MRS. JANE: Youngest daughter of the late Rev. Mr. Bates of Highbury, who marries Lieutenant Fairfax and on his death in action, dies soon afterwards of consumption and grief, leaving a daughter, Jane, aged three. *Emma*

FAIRFAX, JANE: Only granddaughter of Mrs. Bates, three years old when orphaned, and at first brought up by her grandmother and aunt Miss Bates, in reduced circumstances in Highbury. However, when Colonel Campbell returns to England he takes an interest in her out of friendship and gratitude towards her father, and takes her into his own home before she is nine to be brought up with his daughter. Educated to become a governess, she is too much beloved to be parted with, until Miss Campbell marries. At twenty-one she visits Highbury before seeking work. During a trip to Weymouth she has become secretly engaged to Frank Churchill, who is dependent on his capricious aunt, but his visits to Highbury make disguise and concealment very burdensome, especially his pretence of flirting with Emma. She breaks off the engagement, and yields to Mrs. Elton's officious pressure to become governess to Mrs. Smallridge. The sudden death of Frank Churchill's aunt brings him independence and removes misunderstandings, and they marry and go to live in Yorkshire. A very accomplished, remarkably elegant girl with dark hair, grey eyes and a pale complexion, she is not befriended by her contemporary, Emma Woodhouse, who attributes her own rather jealous coolness to Jane's impenetrable reserve. *Emma*

FANNY: Colonel Brandon's cousin, not yet married. *Sense and Sensibility*

FERRARS, MRS.: Widow of a man who died very rich, she is in control of her children's fortunes. A little thin woman, she is upright, even to formality, in her figure, and serious, even to sourness, in her aspect. Naturally expressionless, 'a lucky contraction of the brow had rescued her countenance from the disgrace of insipidity, by giving it the strong character of pride and ill-nature'. Ambitious for her diffident elder son Edward, she snubs Elinor Dashwood whose love for him she suspects, by pointedly preferring the humble Lucy Steele—who in fact is secretly engaged to him herself. Learning this, she is appalled and disinherits him, but when Lucy then elopes with her favourite younger son she is both more afflicted and more forgiving. Though still annoyed at Edward's immediate engagement to Elinor, she is resigned to it as a lesser evil, and makes over to them a respectable income, but, though Lucy's flatteries soon win Robert his mother's favour, Edward is never reinstated as his mother's heir. *Sense and Sensibility*

FERRARS, EDWARD: Elder son of a man who died very rich, but whose fortune depends on the will of his mother, who with his sister is very anxious for him to make a fine figure in the world. His own wishes however centre on domestic comfort and the quiet of private life, and he thanks heaven he cannot be forced into genius and eloquence. Not handsome and rather diffident, his shyness conceals an open affectionate heart. When his sister and her husband inherit Norland, he meets there her sister-in-law Elinor Dashwood and falls in love with her, but his reserve is increased by his secret, now regretted engagement to Lucy Steele, contracted four years ago after his private education at her uncle's house. The secret escapes and Edward is disinherited: he becomes a clergyman, and Elinor is asked by Colonel Brandon to offer him a church living that will enable him to marry her rival. Unexpectedly he is released by Lucy's elopement with his younger brother Robert, and at once he asks Elinor to marry him. His mother, resentful but resigned, grants him a comfortable though not generous income. His honourable fulfilment of obligations, so unlike Willoughby, brings its reward in his curtailed inheritance, for his new profession and reduced expectations bring him far more happiness than his former idle luxury. *Sense and Sensibility*

FERRARS, ROBERT: Has a person and face of strong, natural, sterling insignificance, though adorned in the first style of fashion. A coxcomb, familiar and conceited in manner, a total contrast with his diffident brother Edward, which he attributes to his own public school education. When Edward, being engaged to the unsuitable Lucy Steele, is disinherited in his favour, he is confident of persuading her to renounce his brother, but ends by eloping with her himself. 'Proud of his conquest, proud of tricking Edward, and very proud of marrying privately without his mother's consent,' he is soon forgiven by his capricious mother, and far from being disinherited in his turn, he retains his larger fortune and prospects. *Sense and Sensibility*

FITZWILLIAM, COLONEL: Younger son of an earl, cousin of Mr. Darcy with whom he visits their aunt Lady Catherine de Bourgh, and joint guardian with him of Miss Darcy. About thirty, not handsome, but in person and address most truly the gentleman. Elizabeth Bennett who is staying nearby catches his fancy very much, but he hints that he has to marry a rich woman. *Pride and Prejudice*

FLETCHER, SAM: A friend of John Thorpe, with whom he intends to hire a house in Leicestershire for hunting, has a horse to sell. *Northanger Abbey*

FORD, MRS.: Of Ford's shop, woollen drapers, linen drapers and haberdashers combined, the first in size and fashion in the village, quite an institution in Highbury. Mrs. Ford is very obliging. *Emma*

FORSTER, COLONEL: An officer of the militia regiment, quartered at Meryton. Lydia Bennett stays with him and his wife later at Brighton, and when she runs away with Wickham, tries to trace their route, and breaks the news to the Bennetts. A good-hearted, honourable man. *Pride and Prejudice*

35

FORSTER, MRS. HARRIET: A very young woman, marries Colonel Forster and becomes an intimate friend of Lydia Bennett, brought together by their common good humour and high spirits. Invites Lydia to stay with her when the regiment moves to Brighton, and evidently is an inefficient chaperon. *Pride and Prejudice*

FRANKLAND, MRS.: She and Lady Alicia describe to Lady Russell certain window curtains in Pulteney Street as the handsomest in Bath. *Persuasion*

FRASER, MR.: Marries Mary Crawford's friend, and turns out ill-tempered and exigent; he wants his beautiful young wife to be as steady as himself. *Mansfield Park*

FRASER, MRS. JANET: Née Ross, sister of Lady Stornaway, an intimate friend of Mary Crawford who nevertheless comes to prefer her Mansfield Park acquaintances. A cold-hearted, vain, beautiful woman of twenty-five, she marries entirely for convenience, after three days' consideration. She insists on gaiety and does not manage her older, rich husband well; this results in unedifying matrimonial irritation of a kind not found at Mansfield. She attributes her disappointment not to faults of judgment but to not being rich enough. Typical of the worst aspects of fashionable town society, she is a determined supporter of everything mercenary and ambitious, provided it be only mercenary and ambitious enough. *Mansfield Park*

FRASER, MARGARET: Daughter of Mr. Fraser by a first marriage, she tries to attract Henry Crawford. *Mansfield Park*

FRASERS, THE LADY: Neighbours of General Tilney, whom he wishes were in the country to contribute to society and entertainment for his guest Catherine Morland —but they are not. *Northanger Abbey*

FREEMAN: A Christchurch man, a very good sort of fellow.

Sells his gig to John Thorpe because he wants cash. *Northanger Abbey*

G

GARDINER, MR.: A sensible, pleasant, well-mannered man, greatly superior to his sister Mrs. Bennett as much by nature as by education. He lives by a respectable trade in London within sight of his own warehouses, and though despised by such fine ladies as Miss Bingley for this, is in fact the most truly gentlemanly of the Bennetts' relations. He does all he can to find Lydia Bennett when she elopes, and is willing to pay the necessary sum to ensure her marriage, though Mr. Darcy prevents this. *Pride and Prejudice*

GARDINER, MRS.: Wife of Mr. Gardiner, several years younger than her sisters-in-law, an amiable, intelligent, elegant woman, a great favourite with her nieces the Bennett sisters, especially the two eldest, At one time she lived in Derbyshire near the home of Mr. Darcy, and their tour in that district is the means of reintroducing him to Elizabeth Bennett. She has four children. *Pride and Prejudice*

GIBSON, OLD: Used to live at East Kingham Farm which is later bought by John Dashwood. *Sense and Sensibility*

GILBERTS, THE TWO: Two young men invited to Mr. Weston's ball. Also MISS GILBERT, their sister, and MRS. GILBERT, their mother, who does not mean to dance even with her old acquaintance Mr. Elton. *Emma*

GILBERTS, THE: Cannot be invited to dine with the Middletons (and increase the family party from a mere eight) because it is their turn to invite the Middletons. *Sense and Sensibility*

GODBY, MISS: An acquaintance of the Steeles. *Sense and Sensibility*

GODDARD, MRS.: The mistress of an unpretentious, real, honest, old-fashioned Boarding School where a reasonable quantity of accomplishments are sold at a reasonable price. A 'plain motherly kind of woman, who had worked hard in her youth and now thought herself entitled to the occasional holiday of a tea-visit'. On one of these visits she introduces her pupil Harriet Smith to Emma Woodhouse. *Emma*

GOULDINGS, THE: They live at Haye-Park and dine with the Bennetts. William drives a curricle. *Pride and Prejudice*

GRANTLEY, MISS: A young lady whose design for a table Miss Bingley considers greatly inferior to Miss Darcy's. *Pride and Prejudice*

GRAHAM, MR.: A friend of Mr. John Knightly who intends to have a bailiff from Scotland to look after his new estate. *Emma*

GRANT, DR.: Succeeds Mr. Norris as Rector of Mansfield. He is a hearty man of forty-five, a 'short-necked, apoplectic sort of fellow', a stay-at-home man who likes to be entertained by his sister-in-law Mary Crawford. She considers him, though really a gentleman, a good scholar, clever and very respectable, but also an indolent, selfish *bon vivant*, who must have his palate consulted in everything and who, if the cook makes a blunder, is out of humour with his excellent wife. He is unexpectedly made a dean of Westminster, where he brings on an apoplexy and death by three great institutional dinners in one week. *Mansfield Park*

GRANT, MRS.: Wife of Dr. Grant, a kind, good-natured woman of about thirty, dowered with only five thousand pounds, half-sister to the Crawfords. She takes pains to arrange household comforts for her demanding husband, and after his death lives with Mary Crawford, benefiting her by true kindness and rational tranquillity. With a temperament to love and be loved and a happy disposition, she leaves Mansfield with regret but finds contentment in her new home. *Mansfield Park*

GRAY'S: Mr. Gray's shop in Sackville Street, a fashionable jeweller's. *Sense and Sensibility*

GREEN, MR.: Gives a dinner in Bath at which Mr. Elton and Miss Hawkins further their acquaintance. *Emma*

GREEN, MR.: Mrs. Norris talks to him about Lady Bertram's dairymaid. *Mansfield Park*

GREGORYS, THE: Childhood friends of the Prices in Portsmouth, grown up amazingly fine girls, but because one of them, LUCY, is courted by a lieutenant, will now hardly speak to William Price, who is only a midshipman. *Mansfield Park*

GREY, MISS SOPHIA: An heiress with fifty thousand pounds, a smart stylish girl but not handsome, is known by Willoughby to be ready to marry him, so that he has a motive for jilting Marianne Dashwood and courting her. Jealous, though knowing of his lack of regard for her, she intercepts a note from Marianne and dictates his reply breaking off their acquaintance. *Sense and Sensibility*

GRIERSON, LADY MARY: Captain Wentworth just misses giving her and her daughters a passage on his ship from Lisbon, which, as he disapproves of women on shipboard, he considers a lucky escape. *Persuasion*

GROOM, JOHN: Mrs. Norris has promised him to write to Mrs. Jefferies about his son, and he waits half an hour for her to do so. (Groom is more probably his occupation than his name.) *Mansfield Park*

H

HAGGERSTON: Mr. Gardiner's lawyer, prepares Lydia Bennett's marriage settlement. *Pride and Prejudice*

HANNAH: Daughter of James the coachman, whose master Mr. Woodhouse recommends her as housemaid to Mrs. Weston at Randalls. A civil, pretty-spoken, respectful girl. *Emma*

HARDING, MR.: An old and most particular friend of Sir Thomas Bertram who writes to warn him of his daughter Mrs. Rushworth's flirtation with Henry Crawford and then reports their elopement. He is thwarted by the elder Mrs. Rushworth in his efforts to prevent a scandal. *Mansfield Park*

HARRINGTONS, THE TWO: Friends of the younger Bennetts, invited to the Forsters for a little dance, but HARRIET is ill so PEN has to come alone. *Pride and Prejudice*

HARRIS, MR.: The Palmers' apothecary, attends their guest Marianne Dashwood when her feverish cold turns into serious illness. *Sense and Sensibility*

HARRISON, COLONEL: At Fanny's first ball he says the finest young man in the room is Mr. Crawford or William Price, Lady Bertram cannot recollect which. *Mansfield Park*

HARRY: Servant of Mr. Knightly, whom Mrs. Elton would not have standing at her sideboard for any consideration. *Emma*

HARVILLE, CAPTAIN: A tall dark man with a sensible benevolent countenance, naturally of a serious, thoughtful expression, from strong features and want of health looking much older than his friend Captain Wentworth, whose manners he does not equal, though unaffected, warm and obliging. Never really well since a severe wound two years before, he settles for the winter at Lyme, where Wentworth brings a party of Uppercross friends on a visit, during which Louisa Musgrove falls and injures her head, and is taken to the Harvilles' lodgings. *Persuasion*

HARVILLE, MRS.: A degree less polished than her husband but with the same good feelings. When Louisa Musgrove is injured near their lodgings she willingly takes her in and, being a very experienced nurse, looks after her. She has a sister and cousin, conveyed by Captain Wentworth from Portsmouth to Plymouth. *Persuasion*

HARVILLES, THE LITTLE: The Harvilles' children, three mentioned as accompanying their mother from Portsmouth to Plymouth. *Persuasion*

HARVILLE, FANNY: Captain Harville's sister, a very superior woman, engaged to Captain Benwick, but dies before their marriage. *Persuasion*

HAYTER, MR.: Owner of Winthrop, has some property, though insignificant compared with Mr. Musgrove's. *Persuasion*

HAYTER, MRS.: Sister of Mrs. Musgrove, has also had money but marries a poorer man. Their way of living is inferior, retired and unpolished. *Persuasion*

HAYTER, CHARLES: Eldest son of the Hayters, who chooses to be a scholar and a gentleman, and is very superior in cultivation and manners to the rest. He is a non-resident curate, and has an understanding with his cousin Henrietta Musgrove, interrupted by her temporary attraction for Captain Wentworth. His withdrawal rekindles her affection and they become engaged, and when he is unexpectedly asked to hold a rich church living for some years, they are able to marry. *Persuasion*

HAYTERS, THE MISS: Cousins of the Musgroves, much poorer but with no pride on either side. Are admitted to the honour of being in love with Captain Wentworth. *Persuasion*

HAWKINS, MISS AUGUSTA: *see* Elton, Mrs.

HENRY, SIR: A guest of Lord Ravenshaw's houseparty, where he covets the duke's part in their amateur theatricals. He is thought 'such a stick' by Mr. Yates. *Mansfield Park*

HENSHAWE, BIDDY: Aunt of Sophia Grey who marries Willoughby. Known to Mrs. Jennings, married to a very wealthy man. *Sense and Sensibility*

HILL, MRS.: Mrs. Bennett's housekeeper. *Pride and Prejudice*

HODGES, THE: They persuade Isabella Thorpe to attend a half-price play, which she accepts to avoid their teasing on her loss of Captain Tilney. *Northanger Abbey*

HODGES, CHARLES: Isabella Thorpe anticipates his teasing and conjectures when she refuses to dance during James Morland's absence. *Northanger Abbey*

HODGES, MRS.: Mr. Knightly's housekeeper at Donwell Abbey, sometimes cross, is annoyed at his giving away his last apples to the Bates'. *Emma*

HOLFORD, MRS.: An acquaintance of Tom Bertram, at whose house he is embarrassed by Miss Anderson. *Mansfield Park*

HUGHES, DR.: Present at Mr. Weston's ball, known to Miss Bates, also his wife MRS. HUGHES, and MR. RICHARD, probably their son. *Emma*

HUGHES, MRS.: An acquaintance of Mrs. Thorpe, accompanies Miss Tilney to a Bath assembly. *Northanger Abbey*

HUNT, CAPTAIN: Miss Thorpe tells him at one of their winter assemblies that she will not dance with him unless he admits Miss Andrews is as beautiful as an angel. *Northanger Abbey*

HURST, MR.: Husband of Mr. Bingley's sister, an indolent man of more fashion than fortune, lives only to eat, drink and play at cards. *Pride and Prejudice*

HURST, MRS. LOUISA: Née Bingley. Fashionable and a very fine lady, likes to economise by considering her brother's house her home. *Pride and Prejudice*

I

IBBOTSONS, THE: People of note in Bath. *Persuasion*

J

JACKSON: Of Oriel, bids sixty guineas for John Thorpe's gig and horse. *Northanger Abbey*

JAMES: Mr. Woodhouse's coachman, highly depended upon. Exertion is spared him and his horses, wherever possible. Has a daughter Hannah. *Emma*

JEFFEREYS, MRS.: Mrs. Elton's provinciality appears in describing her as 'Clara Partridge that was' when she is unlikely to be known under either name outside her own circle. She is instanced as a musical young lady who gives up music after marriage. *Emma*

JEFFERIES, MRS.: Mrs. Norris writes to her about John Groom's son. *Mansfield Park*

JEMIMA: Mary Musgrove's nursery maid, who to Mary is the truest, steadiest creature in the world, and to the elder

Mrs. Musgrove is 'always upon the gad' and 'such a fine-dressing lady that she is enough to ruin any servants she comes near'. *Persuasion*

JENKINSON, MRS.: Miss Anne de Bourgh's companion, attends to her incessantly. *Pride and Prejudice*

JENNINGS, MR.: Mrs. Jennings' late husband, who after trading with success in a less elegant part of town, dies eight years before she meets the Dashwoods. *Sense and Sensibility*

JENNINGS, MRS.: Mother of Lady Middleton and Mrs. Palmer. A good-humoured, merry, fat elderly woman, who talks a great deal, seems very happy and rather vulgar. Fond of matchmaking and teasing young girls about their admirers, she invites Elinor and Marianne Dashwood to stay with her in London, which the latter, though particularly irritated by her, eagerly accepts, believing Willoughby to be in London. Mrs. Jennings is very sympathetic when Marianne is jilted, and both sisters are invited to accompany her to visit Mrs. Palmer: there her untiring and expert nursing of Marianne's dangerous fever, together with her kindness, make Elinor really love her. *Sense and Sensibility*

JOHN: The Collins' manservant. *Pride and Prejudice*

JOHN: The Gardiners' manservant, accompanies them on their tour of Derbyshire. *Pride and Prejudice*

JONES, MR.: Apothecary at Meryton, attends Jane Bennett when she catches a bad cold and has to stay at Netherfield. *Pride and Prejudice*

K

KING, MR.: Master of Ceremonies at the Lower Rooms in Bath. *Northanger Abbey*

KING, MISS MARY: A Meryton young lady, who is not noticed by Mr. Wickham until she inherits ten thousand pounds, when he pays her marked attention. She is sent to stay with an uncle in Liverpool to be out of his way. A very good sort of girl to some, a nasty little freckled thing to others. *Pride and Prejudice*

KNIGHTLEY, MR. GEORGE: Owner of Donwell Abbey, the most considerable estate in the country, though not otherwise wealthy, connected with Emma Woodhouse whose sister is married to his brother. A thoughtful man of about seven or eight and thirty, he has a sensible, frank manner that rises above trivial irritations, but is kind, considerate and tactful. The only person who ever criticises Emma, he is angry that she influences Harriet Smith against his protégé Robert Martin, and reprimands her disrespectful witticisms at the garrulous Miss Bates' expense. The high value he sets on honesty and openness influences him against Frank Churchill, who equivocates a little, but his real animus derives from jealousy of Frank's attentions to Emma; when reassured that she has never returned these, he proposes to her himself; and rather than distress the frail Mr. Woodhouse, he decides to move to her house. Though Emma deplores his unceremonious indifference to rank, his usual generous conduct is guided by disregard for all pettiness. *Emma*

KNIGHTLEY, JOHN: Younger brother of George Knightley, he marries Emma Woodhouse's sister Isabella. A tall, gentleman-like, very clever man, a successful lawyer, he is fond of domesticity and is reserved in manner, even occasionally irritable, which his wife's yielding temper encourages. Occasionally impatient with Mr. Woodhouse's hypochondria, critical of Emma, and amazed by Mr. Weston's sociability. He greets Emma's engagement to his brother with moderate if sincere congratulations. *Emma*

KNIGHTLEY, MRS. ISABELLA: Emma Woodhouse's elder

sister, married to John Knightley, lives in London and has five children. A pretty, elegant little woman of gentle, quiet manners, and a disposition remarkably amiable and affectionate; a devoted wife, a doting mother, and tenderly attached to her father and sister. Not, however, a woman of strong understanding or any quickness, she has always been less clever than her younger sister. She is almost as concerned about caring for her family's health as her father. *Emma*

KNIGHTLEY CHILDREN, THE: Five children of John and Isabella Knightley—Henry, John, Isabella, George and Emma. *Emma*

L

LARKINS, WILLIAM: Employed by Mr. Knightley and is his right-hand man on his estate, Donwell Abbey, and thinks more of his master's profit than anything. He is an old acquaintance of Miss Bates. He becomes annoyed when Mr. Knightley is too occupied with his secret engagement to Emma Woodhouse to attend to business. *Emma*

LASCELLES, LADY: Previously occupied one of the best houses in Wimpole Street, which is later acquired by Mrs. Rushworth. *Mansfield Park*

LEE, MISS: Governess to Maria and Julia Bertram, later also to Fanny Price, at whose ignorance she wonders. *Mansfield Park*

LONG, MRS.: A neighbour of Mrs. Bennett who brings the first news of Mr. Bingley's residence at Netherfield. She does not keep a carriage. She has two nieces, who are very pretty behaved girls and not at all handsome. *Pride and Prejudice*

LONGTOWN, THE MARQUIS OF: General Tilney is disappointed in hopes of seeing him at Bath; the General later decides to visit him with his family in Herefordshire on the spur of the moment, as some excuse for turning Catherine Morland out of his own house. *see also* Alice (Lady?). *Northanger Abbey*

LUCAS, CHARLOTTE: Eldest daughter of Sir William Lucas, a sensible but plain woman of seven and twenty, an intimate friend of Elizabeth Bennett. Without thinking highly either of men or of matrimony, marriage has always been her object, and when Mr. Collins is refused by Elizabeth, she attracts his attentions to herself and accepts him from the pure and disinterested desire of an establishment. Her one regret is the loss of Elizabeth's esteem by this mercenary move. She guides and puts up with her husband very well. *Pride and Prejudice*

LUCAS, MARIA: A younger sister of Charlotte, a friend of Kitty Bennett. She, her father and Elizabeth Bennett visit Charlotte after her marriage, where, not being used to company, she is greatly over-awed by Lady Catherine de Bourgh. *Pride and Prejudice*

LUCAS, SIR WILLIAM: Formerly in trade at Meryton, where he makes a tolerable fortune and becomes mayor. He delivers an address to the king and is knighted, a distinction he feels perhaps too strongly. Gives up trade, moves to Lucas Lodge and occupies himself solely in being civil to all the world. In spite of his constant references to the Court at St. James's, when visiting his married daughter Charlotte he is considerably overawed by her neighbour, Lady Catherine de Bourgh. 'By nature inoffensive, friendly and obliging, his presentation at St. James's had made him courteous.' *Pride and Prejudice*

LUCAS, LADY: Wife of Sir William, a very good kind of

woman, not too clever to be a valuable neighbour to Mrs. Bennett. Has several children. *Pride and Prejudice*

LUCAS, A YOUNG: Younger brother of Charlotte, juvenile enough to argue with Mrs. Bennett on her own terms. *Pride and Prejudice*

M

MACKENZIE: The gardener at Kellynch Hall—probably, as was traditional, Scottish. *Persuasion*

MACLEAN, LADY MARY: An old lady who never misses a Bath concert, and sits in the grand seats around the orchestra. *Persuasion*

MADDISON: Acts for Henry Crawford on his estate at Everingham as steward or agent. A clever fellow, he is suspected of putting his hard-hearted, griping cousin into a mill instead of the honest tenant Henry wants. *Mansfield Park*

MADDOX, CHARLES: A quiet-looking, gentlemanly young man, considered for the part of Anhalt in the Mansfield Park production of *Lovers' Vows*. *Mansfield Park*

MADDOXES, THE MISS: Lady Bertram can not recall what she heard about one of them at Fanny's ball. *Mansfield Park*

MARSHALL, CAPTAIN: William Price's Captain when he is a midshipman. *Mansfield Park*

MARTIN, MRS.: Mother of Robert Martin of Abbey Mill Farm, has *two* parlours and is very kind to Harriet Smith, whom she wishes to marry her son. *Emma*

MARTIN, ELIZABETH: A friend of Harriet Smith at Miss

Goddard's school, invites her to stay at her home, whereupon her brother Robert falls in love with Harriet. He is
upset when he is refused, and has to struggle still to appear
friendly. Also MARTIN, MISS: her sister, also at Miss
Goddard's school. *Emma*

MARTIN, ROBERT: Farmer at Abbey Mill Farm, a neat,
sensible young man of twenty-four though awkward and
abrupt in manner. He loves Harriet Smith and is refused
by her through Emma Woodhouse's influence, but after
she is disappointed in more ambitious aspirations, he is
accepted at the second time of asking. Highly regarded by
Mr. Knightley. *Emma*

MARY: The maid at Mrs. Smith's lodgings. *Persuasion*

MATILDA: A fictional creation of Henry Tilney's, the
discovery of whose memoirs forms the climax of his teasing
picture of what awaits Catherine Morland at Northanger
Abbey. *Northanger Abbey*

MAXWELL, MRS. ADMIRAL: Godmother to Mary Price to
whom she gives a silver knife. *Mansfield Park*

METCALFE, LADY: An acquaintance of Lady Catherine de
Bourgh who recommends to her a chance-mentioned
governess. She calls to thank Lady Catherine for giving her
'a treasure'. *Pride and Prejudice*

MIDDLETON, SIR JOHN: A good-looking man, about forty,
a sportsman who otherwise employs his time in collecting
about him more young people than his house will hold, and
the noisier they are, the better is he pleased. He shows the
real satisfaction of a good heart in finding a nearby cottage
for his relations, the Dashwoods, and welcoming them
there. An honest man, he is enraged by Willoughby's
jilting Marianne Dashwood. *Sense and Sensibility*

MIDDLETON, LADY (MARY): Née Jennings. Not more

than six or seven and twenty, she has a handsome face, a tall and striking figure, and all the elegance of manner that her husband lacks, but she lacks his frankness and warmth. Reserved, cold and correct, she overlooks Willoughby's jilting her relation Marianne Dashwood because he and his bride are rich and fashionable. By occupation a mother, she humours her children constantly. Her mother Mrs. Jennings says she always gets her own way. *Sense and Sensibility*

MIDDLETONS, THE FOUR YOUNG: JOHN, the eldest, WILLIAM, the second, and ANNAMARIA, a little girl of three; and another. *Sense and Sensibility*

MILLAR, COLONEL: An officer whose regiment is quartered near Mrs. Bennett's home when she is a young girl. *Pride and Prejudice*

MITCHELL, FARMER: His umbrellas are gallantly borrowed by Mr. Weston for Emma and her governess Miss Taylor. *Emma*

MITCHELLS, THE: Are not to be at the ball which Isabella Thorpe continuously congratulates herself on not attending. They later show possibly insincere surprise and friendship when Isabella has lost both her suitors. *Northanger Abbey*

MITCHELL, ANNE: One of the Mitchells; she copies a turban worn by Isabella Thorpe. *Northanger Abbey*

MOLLAND'S: A shop in Milsom Street, Bath. *Persuasion*

MORLAND, CATHERINE: Fourth child and eldest daughter of the Rev. Richard Morland's large family. She grows from a careless, romping child into a rather pretty girl of seventeen with an affectionate heart, a cheerful, open disposition, 'and her mind about as ignorant and un-informed as the female mind at seventeen usually is'. She is taken by her neighbours, the Allens, to Bath where she meets Isabella Thorpe who becomes her friend, gets engaged to her brother, James Morland, and introduces her to the delightful terrors of the Gothic horror novel; later, when Catherine meets and falls in love with Henry Tilney, and is invited by her sister Eleanor to stay with them, she is delighted to find they live in Northanger Abbey, a likely setting for ghosts and horrors. She imagines that General Tilney, her friends' father, has murdered or locked away his wife, and when this is understood and refuted by Henry she is deeply ashamed and resolves to be sensible; however, adventure strikes in a mundane form when the General, indignant at his own over-estimation of Catherine's wealth and eligibility, vents his anger by sending her home at a moment's notice, without escort or courtesy. Her unhappiness is soon assuaged by Henry's visit, proposing to marry her in spite of his father, and when at length the General's consent is won (for she is not penniless and will have three thousand pounds), they marry and are happy. Although credulous and imaginative enough to be strongly affected both by the insincere Isabella Thorpe and the improbabilities of the horror novel, Catherine's real generosity, good principles and her own open sincerity preserve her from their influence. *Northanger Abbey*

MORLAND, GEORGE and HARRIET: A younger brother and sister of Catherine, probably the youngest of the family aged six and four, who expect a brother or sister in every coach that arrives. *Northanger Abbey*

MORLAND, JAMES: Eldest of the Morlands' children, up at Oxford, he is to be a clergyman. He is a friend of John Thorpe, whose sister Isabella he falls in love with. Meeting her again when she becomes the friend of his sister Catherine in Bath, he becomes engaged to her. However, she has imagined him much richer than he is, and hearing what money his father can give him, breaks their engagement in hopes of doing better. Very fond of Catherine, he is not a good judge of character, and his parents hope his disappointment will ultimately be for the best. *Northanger Abbey*

MORLAND, MR. RICHARD: A clergyman, father of Catherine and nine other children. Not well equipped as a heroine's father, for he is neither neglected nor poor: 'a very respectable man, though his name was Richard,' and not in the least addicted to locking up his daughters. When his eldest son James wishes to marry, he plans to give up a generous portion of his income to him. *Northanger Abbey*

MORLAND, MRS.: A woman of useful plain sense, with a good temper and good constitution, her time occupied with lying-in and giving their early education to her ten children. *Northanger Abbey*

MORLAND, RICHARD: One of the Morlands' sons, whose cravats Catherine sews, or more often neglects, in her unhappiness after returning from Northanger. *Northanger Abbey*

MORLAND, SARAH (SALLY): Catherine's next sister, a girl of sixteen—does *not* demand her sister write by every post during her visit to Bath. *Northanger Abbey*

MORLAND FAMILY, THE: Mr. and Mrs. Morland's ten children: 'a family of ten children will always be called a fine family, where there are heads and arms and legs enough for the number.' *Northanger Abbey*

MORLEY, SIR BASIL: A friend of Sir Walter Elliot. *Persuasion*

MORRIS, MR.: Mr. Bingley comes to an agreement with him about renting Netherfield; the owner or the owner's agent. *Pride and Prejudice*

MORTON, LORD: Now dead, father of Miss Morton. *Sense and Sensibility*

MORTON, THE HON. MISS: Daughter of the late Lord Morton, has thirty thousand pounds. Mrs. Ferrars wishes her to marry her son Edward. *Sense and Sensibility*

MUSGROVE, MR. CHARLES (THE ELDER): Owner of Uppercross-Hall, second in importance only to Sir Walter Elliot in their neighbourhood. Friendly, hearty and hospitable, not much educated and not at all elegant. A good father. *Persuasion*

MUSGROVE, MRS.: Wife of Mr. Musgrove, a kind, old-fashioned woman, of substantial size, infinitely more fitted by nature to express good cheer and good humour than tenderness and sentiment. Her heartiness, warmth and sincerity are a pleasant change from the Elliots' cold civility. *Persuasion*

MUSGROVE, CHARLES: Eldest son and heir of Mr. Musgrove, a civil agreeable young man, he wishes to marry Anne Elliot; when refused by her he marries her younger sister Mary, to whom he is superior in sense and temper, so that she does not improve and refine his character as a wife of real understanding might have. He does nothing with much zeal but sport, and otherwise trifles his time away. Of good spirits, he is an affectionate husband and brother. *Persuasion*

MUSGROVE, MRS. MARY: Youngest daughter of Sir Walter, marries Charles Musgrove after he is refused by her sister Anne. In person inferior to both her sisters, and far beneath Anne in understanding and temper, she is yet not so repulsive and unsisterly as Elizabeth: when well and properly attended to she has great good humour, but is always imagining ailments through selfishness and idleness. She never forgets her rank as a baronet's daughter. She manages her children very badly. *Persuasion*

MUSGROVE, CHARLES (LITTLE): Elder child of Charles

and Mary Musgrove, injures his back and shoulder in a fall. *Persuasion*

MUSGROVE, HARRY: The youngest, lingering and long-petted Musgrove son, who at last goes to school. *Persuasion*

MUSGROVE, HENRIETTA: The Musgroves' elder daughter, a pleasant, unaffected girl of twenty, educated at a school in Exeter, living to be fashionable, happy and merry. Rather prettier and gentler than her sister, she has an understanding with her cousin Charles Hayter and after wavering in favour of Captain Wentworth she becomes engaged to Hayter, and when he is given a good Church living, they marry. *Persuasion*

MUSGROVE, LOUISA: Second daughter of the Musgroves, a pretty unaffected girl of nineteen, higher spirited than her sister. Praised by Captain Wentworth for her firmness, she carries it to the point of headstrong obstinacy and, persisting in jumping from high steps, falls and injures her head. Her slow recovery in the house of the Harvilles results in her falling in love with their guest Captain Benwick; more delicate now, the high-spirited, joyous, talking Louisa Musgrove is transformed into a suitable match for the dejected, thinking, feeling, reading Captain Benwick. This releases Wentworth, who has unintentionally raised expectations of attachment to her. *Persuasion*

MUSGROVE, RICHARD (DICK): A very troublesome, hopeless son of the Musgroves, sent to sea because he is stupid and unmanageable on shore; is very little cared for at any time by his family, though quite as much as he deserves, seldom heard of, and scarcely at all regretted when he dies abroad, aged twenty, until memory much later arouses fresh sorrow in his mother. As a midshipman spends six months on board the *Laconia*, the ship of Captain Wentworth, who is thus known to the Musgroves. *Persuasion*

MUSGROVE, WALTER: Younger son of Charles and Mary

54

Musgrove, a remarkable stout, forward child of two years old. *Persuasion*

MUSGROVES, THE YOUNG: Mr. and Mrs. Musgrove's other numerous children, not yet grown up. *Persuasion*

N

NANNY: Mrs. Norris' servant and 'chief counsellor', is to go to London to escort the child Fanny Price, first travelling from Portsmouth to Mansfield Park, destined by her miserly mistress to sleep and meet Fanny at her cousin the saddler's house. Sir Thomas substitutes a more respectable though less economical rendezvous. *Mansfield Park*

NASH, MISS: Headteacher at Miss Goddard's school, has a sister well married to a linen draper. *Emma*

NICHOLLS, MRS.: Mr. Bingley's housekeeper at Netherfield. *Pride and Prejudice*

NORRIS, THE REV.: A friend of Sir Thomas Bertram whose sister-in-law Miss Ward he marries. He has scarcely any private fortune but Sir Thomas gives him a living at Mansfield. He later becomes ill with gouty complaints, and dies. His wife consoles herself 'by considering that she could do very well without him'. *Mansfield Park*

NORRIS, MRS.: Née Ward. Elder sister of Lady Bertram, though as handsome and well-dowered has to accept a mere clergyman, her brother-in-law's friend, and settles in the parsonage close to her sister's home, until widowed when she moves to a smaller house nearby. Of a managing, officious disposition, she is also uncharitable and miserly, so her activity is limited to whatever costs no money. Her favourites are her nieces Maria and Julia whom she confirms in conceit and self-indulgence by her partiality, but she dislikes the Bertrams' protégée Fanny Price, her niece, whose life she makes a misery by her scolding and uncomfortable economies. She promotes Maria's marriage to the rich, stupid Mr. Rushworth, and tries to excuse her later adultery with Henry Crawford, afterwards going to live with her in disgraced retirement, where their tempers become their mutual punishment. Devoid of generosity and judgment, she becomes a thorn in Sir Thomas's flesh—she seems 'a part of himself that must be born forever', and her departure purifies Mansfield Park of its taint of worldliness and materialism. *Mansfield Park*

O

OLIVER, TOM: A very clever fellow, considered for the part of Anhalt in the Mansfield Park theatricals. Another OLIVER, his brother. *Mansfield Park*

OTWAYS, THE: Present at Mr. Weston's ball, including MR. and MRS. OTWAY, MISS OTWAY, MISS CAROLINE, MR. GEORGE and MR. ARTHUR. *Emma*

OWEN, MR.: Son of a clergyman, a friend of Edmund Bertram, living at Lessingby near Peterborough. Edmund visits him just before they are both ordained. *Mansfield Park*

OWENS, THE MISS: Sisters of Mr. Owen. Three are grown up, pleasant, good-humoured, unaffected girls though not equal to Mary Crawford or Fanny Price. *Mansfield Park*

P

PALMER, MR. THOMAS: Owner of Cleveland, husband of Mrs. Jennings' daughter Charlotte. He affects incivility bordering on rudeness as a means of distinguishing himself in company, though as he hopes to enter Parliament he has to go about his own neighbourhood making everyone like him. However, in his own house he is perfectly the gentleman to his visitors and only occasionally rude to his wife and her mother, very capable of being a pleasant companion, were he not inclined to fancy himself superior to people in general. *Sense and Sensibility*

PALMER, MRS. CHARLOTTE: Mrs. Jennings' younger and favourite daughter, totally unlike her sister Lady Middleton, being short, plump, very pretty and very good-humoured; 'her kindness recommended by so pretty a face, was engaging; her folly, though evident, was not disgusting, because it was not conceited; and Elinor could have forgiven anything but her laugh.' She gives birth to a son. *Sense and Sensibility*

PARRYS, THE: An acquaintance of the Allens, who do not come to Bath as they talked of once, which Mrs. Allen regrets as George Parry could dance with her partnerless guest, Catherine Morland. *Northanger Abbey*

PARRYS, THE: They and the Sandersons are to come to Mrs. Jenning's house the evening that Marianne Dashwood learns of Willoughby's fickleness. *Sense and Sensibility*

PARTRIDGE, MRS.: A particular friend of Mrs. Elton, with whom she always resides when in Bath (Emma Woodhouse guesses her to be a vulgar, dashing widow). *Emma*

PATTY: The Bates' only servant, who makes an excellent apple dumpling. *Emma*

PERRY, MR.: Apothecary at Highbury, attends most of its inhabitants as physician, and is greatly depended upon by Mr. Woodhouse. He is bilious and has not time to take care of himself. *Emma*

PERRY, MRS.: Wife of Mr. Perry, who on the pretext of his health wishes him to set up his own carriage. *Emma*

PERRYS, THE LITTLE: Children of Mr. Perry. Their possession of slices of Mr. Weston's indigestible wedding cake suggests the family's robust private attitude to health. *Emma*

PHILLIPS, MR.: An attorney at Meryton, once clerk to Mrs. Bennett's father, marries her sister and succeeds to the business. Broad-faced, stuffy and breathing port wine, he is hospitable and his visits to the officers of the militia quartered in Meryton is a means of introducing them to his nieces, the Miss Bennetts. *Pride and Prejudice*

PHILLIPS, MRS.: Sister of Mrs. Bennett, a kindly, gossiping, inquisitive woman, rather vulgar. She holds boisterous supper parties, has a familiar manner and, fond of her nieces the Miss Bennetts, is very anxious for them to get husbands. *Pride and Prejudice*

POOLES, THE: Mary Musgrove dines with them. *Persuasion*

POPE, MISS: A young governess, mentioned by chance to Lady Catherine de Bourgh who recommends her to Lady Metcalfe: she turns out 'a treasure'. *Pride and Prejudice*

PRATT, MR.: A private tutor, at whose house Edward Ferrars is educated. His niece there meets and becomes engaged to Edward. *Sense and Sensibility*

PRATT: An officer in the militia quartered at Meryton. *Pride and Prejudice*

PRESCOTT, LADY: Notices something, Lady Bertram cannot recollect what, in Fanny at her first ball. *Mansfield Park*

PRICE, MR. (LIEUTENANT): Marries Frances, the youngest sister of Mrs. Norris and Lady Bertram. A Lieutenant of Marines without education, fortune or connections, his career is not a success and eleven years later he is disabled for active service but not the less equal to company and good liquor. When his daughter Fanny revisits her home after eight years he pays little attention to her. Though he swears and he drinks, and is dirty and gross, his behaviour is more restrained and acceptable to strangers. *Mansfield Park*

PRICE, MRS. FRANCES: Née Ward, sister of Lady Bertram and Mrs. Norris, she marries to disoblige her family Lieut. Price of the Marines. A quarrel between the sisters lasts eleven years until Mrs. Price can no longer afford to cherish pride or resentment, and Fanny her eldest daughter is taken in by the Bertrams. Her maternal affection when Fanny visits her eight years later is warm because instinctive but soon satisfied, and her incompetence as a housewife shocks her daughter. A 'partial, ill-judging parent, a dawdle, a slattern, who neither taught nor restrained her children, whose house was the scene of mismanagement and discomfort from beginning to end', she is basically as kindly and indolent as Lady Bertram, without the means to indulge herself. *Mansfield Park*

PRICE, BETSEY: At five, she is the youngest Price and is the first of her daughters that her mother ever much regarded; a spoilt child. *Mansfield Park*

PRICE, CHARLES: At eight, the Prices' youngest son, rosy-faced, ragged and dirty. *Mansfield Park*

PRICE, FANNY: Eldest daughter of Mrs. Price, who having eight other children is thankful to have Fanny brought up in the family of her rich brother-in-law Sir Thomas Bertram. As a timid, humble child of ten, Fanny is overawed by her uncle, scolded by her aunt Norris and patronised by her cousins Maria and Julia Bertram; but her education, less worldly than theirs, inculcates sounder principles. She loves her cousin Edmund, suffering to see him attracted by the witty, worldly Mary Crawford, and refuses the attentions of Henry Crawford whose morals she suspects. Her uncle, annoyed at her refusal, sends her on a visit to her parents' impoverished home to teach her the value of a rich husband. Tried indeed by the discomforts that she is too diffident to ameliorate, Fanny advises and guides her more active sister Susan, but is rescued both from Crawford and Portsmouth by the news of his elopement with Maria which, together with Tom Bertram's grave illness, means she is urgently needed by Lady Bertram. As Edmund is disillusioned by Mary Crawford, she soon consoles him and they are married. Fair, slight and sweet-natured, her modesty, mildness and lack of robustness prevents her acting positively, but she always has the courage to stand by her convictions. *Mansfield Park*

PRICE, JOHN and RICHARD: The Prices' second and third sons, live away from home. *Mansfield Park*

PRICE, MARY: A very pretty little girl, who is about four when Fanny leaves home, and dies a few years later, having given Susan a silver knife which, coveted by Betsey, causes quarrels. *Mansfield Park*

PRICE, SAM: Fanny's brother, a fine, tall boy of eleven years old, loud and overbearing but intelligent, the best of the three younger boys. *Mansfield Park*

PRICE, SUSAN: Fanny's sister, a well-grown girl of fourteen with an open, sensible countenance, bold and determined; her persistence in argument stems not from quarrelsomeness but from an active wish to reform her family's slovenliness. Perceiving her own faults she is eager to learn from Fanny. She has many good principles in spite of her faulty upbringing, and when she is invited to Mansfield Park to comfort and assist Fanny, her more fearless disposition and happier nerves make her useful, and she remains after Fanny's marriage to become perhaps the more beloved of the two. *Mansfield Park*

PRICE, TOM: Nine years old, the brother Fanny has helped to nurse before she leaves her Portsmouth home; he will not suffer patiently her caresses and reminiscences when she returns for a visit. *Mansfield Park*

PRICE, WILLIAM: Fanny's favourite brother, a year older than her, who becomes a sailor. He visits Fanny soon after she leaves home to live at Mansfield Park, just before he first goes to sea. He does so again seven years later, when he meets Henry Crawford who, to ingratiate himself with Fanny, uses influence to get him promoted to Lieutenant. Soon afterwards he takes his sister for her first visit to their parental home but has to sail almost immediately. A young man of open countenance, frank, unstudied but feeling and respectful manners, whose conversation shows good principles, professional knowledge, energy, courage and cheerfulness, he succeeds in his career and makes the idle, rich Henry Crawford envy him. *Mansfield Park*

PRINCE, MISS: A teacher at Miss Goddard's school. *Emma*

R

RAVENSHAW, LORD: Owner of Ecclesford in Cornwall where the large houseparty attended by Mr. Yates prepares to act *Lovers' Vows*. He plays Baron Wildenheim, though a little man with a weak voice. Being one of the most correct men in England he calls off the play upon his grandmother's death. Also **LADY RAVENSHAW**, his wife. *Mansfield Park*

REBECCA: The Prices' upper servant, whose slovenliness and laziness are exacerbated by Mrs. Price's lack of discipline. *Mansfield Park*

REPTON, MR. HUMPHREY: A landscape gardener and well-known 'improver' of estates, he is said to have improved Compton very well for Smith, whose friend Mr. Rushworth then thinks of employing him. His terms are five guineas a day. *Mansfield Park*

REYNOLDS, MRS.: Mr. Darcy's housekeeper at Pemberley, a respectable-looking elderly woman who shows the Gardiners and Elizabeth Bennett round the house. Very much attached to her master and his sister, her praise of his character confirms Elizabeth's improving opinion of him. *Pride and Prejudice*

RICHARD: A servant, to be turned away by Mr. Phillips and hired by Colonel Forster. *Pride and Prejudice*

RICHARD, COUSIN: Cousin of Anne and Lucy Steele, who fears Edward Ferrars will break his engagement with the latter when he is disinherited. *Sense and Sensibility*

RICHARDSON, MISS: A teacher at Miss Goddard's school. *Emma*

RICHARDSONS, THE: Friends of the Steeles; Mrs. Richardson takes Miss Steele in her coach to Kensington Gardens. *Sense and Sensibility*

ROBERT ——, SIR: Uncle of Edward and Robert Ferrars, who persuades their mother against her own judgment to educate Edward privately at Mr. Pratt's home. *Sense and Sensibility*

ROBERT: Mrs. Grant's gardener at Mansfield Parsonage, who will persist in leaving out certain plants on mild autumn nights, ignoring the risk of frost. *Mansfield Park*

ROBINSON, MR.: The apothecary who treats little Charles Musgrove for his injuries. *Persuasion*

ROBINSON, MR.: Asks Mr. Bingley which woman is the prettiest at the Meryton assembly. *Pride and Prejudice*

ROBINSON: Is to be spoken to, so that a cottage which Catherine Morland admires, near Henry Tilney's parsonage, may continue to form part of the view. *Northanger Abbey*

ROOKE, NURSE: Sister of Mrs. Smith's landlady, she nurses her without charge, being out of work, to preserve the boarding house's good name. A shrewd, intelligent, sensible woman, her observations on human nature interest Mrs. Smith, whom she also teaches to knit. *Persuasion*

ROSS, FLORA and JANET: *see* Stornaway, Lady and Fraser, Mrs. Janet

ROSE, MR.: Cited by Miss Steele as 'a prodigious smart young man, quite a beau', clerk to Mr. Simpson of Exeter, but not fit to be seen in the mornings. *Sense and Sensibility*

RUSHWORTH, MR. (THE LATE): A former owner of Sotherton Court, who left off the custom of family prayers in the chapel. May be the younger Mr. Rushworth's father. *Mansfield Park*

RUSHWORTH, MR.: A heavy young man with not more than common sense who succeeds to one of the largest estates and finest places in the country, Sotherton Court. He becomes engaged to Maria Bertram and in spite of discontent and jealousy aroused during the amateur theatricals when she flirts with Henry Crawford, they marry and enter London Society. When she later elopes with Henry Crawford, he easily procures a divorce. Because he marries very much aware of her contempt and preference for another, he deserves his indignity and disappointment. Edmund thinks that 'if this man had not twelve thousand a year, he would be a very stupid fellow'. *Mansfield Park*

RUSHWORTH, MRS. (THE ELDER): Mother of Mr. Rushworth, a well-meaning, civil, prosing, pompous woman, she unites with Mrs. Norris in promoting the marriage of her son and Maria Bertram. Later, when Maria elopes, her bitterness is due to personal disagreements with her as well as resentment for her son. *Mansfield Park*

RUSHWORTH, MRS. MARIA: *see* Bertram, Maria

RUSSELL, SIR HENRY: Lady Russell's late husband. *Persuasion*

RUSSELL, LADY: A widow of steady age and character, she settles near her close friend Lady Elliot whose daughters, after her death, she loves as a mother, especially Anne, her goddaughter. A woman rather of sound than of quick abilities, who combines strict integrity with high respect for rank, benevolent, charitable, and extremely correct in conduct. Shocked by the boldness and wit of Captain Wentworth, she persuades Anne to break off her engagement to him, confident that he is reckless and unreliable. Later she considers the correct and polished manners of Mr. Elliot as evidence of sound principles and wishes him to marry Anne. But loving Anne better than she loves her own abilities she admits her mistakes as regards both men and that she is 'unfairly influenced by appearance in each'. *Persuasion*

S

SADDLER, THE: Cousin of Nanny, servant of Mrs. Norris who regards his house in London as a free lodging for Nanny. *Mansfield Park*

SALLY: The Prices' servant, a girl inferior even to Rebecca. *Mansfield Park*

SALLY: A maid, probably Mrs. Forster's, though possibly Lydia Bennett's, who is to sew up a rent in Lydia's gown before she returns from her elopement. *Pride and Prejudice*

SALLY: One of the maids at Barton Park, whose brother is a post-boy at an Exeter Inn. *Sense and Sensibility*

SANDERSONS, THE: They and the Parrys are to come to Mrs. Jennings' house the evening that Marianne Dashwood learns of Willoughby's fickleness. *Sense and Sensibility*

SARAH: The Musgroves' old nursery maid, with little to do after her last charge goes to school, until she goes to Lyme to nurse the injured Louisa. *Persuasion*

SARAH: One of the Bennetts' maids, helps the young ladies to dress. *Pride and Prejudice*

SAUNDERS, JOHN: Miss Bates intends to take her mother's spectacles to him to mend, but something or another keeps hindering her. *Emma*

SCHOLEY, OLD: A friend of Mr. Price. *Mansfield Park*

SERLE: Servant of Mr. Woodhouse who has absolute confidence in him; he has an inimitable way of boiling pork, not to mention eggs. *Emma*

SHARPE, MARTHA: A friend of Miss Steele. A year or two ago they had secrets together, which Lucy Steele would try to overhear. *Sense and Sensibility*

SIMPSON, MR.: Of Exeter, employer of the smart young Mr. Rose, his clerk. *Sense and Sensibility*

SHEPHERD, MR. JOHN: A civil, courteous lawyer, agent of Sir Walter Elliot at Kellynch, who needs to press him to economise, but who, 'whatever might be his hold or his views on Sir Walter, would rather have the disagreeable prompted by anybody else'. Politely and indirectly persuades him to move to Bath and let Kellynch Hall. *Persuasion*

SHIRLEY, DOCTOR: Rector of Uppercross, who has been zealously discharging his duties for forty years, but is now growing too infirm, especially after his illness a year earlier. He may be persuaded to appoint Charles Hayter his curate, or even to procure a dispensation, leave Uppercross and retire to Lyme, which always makes him feel young again. *Persuasion*

SHIRLEY, MRS.: Wife of Doctor Shirley, has cousins and many acquaintances in Lyme. *Persuasion*

SKINNERS, THE: A family known to the Allens who have been to Bath the previous winter, for the good of Dr. Skinner's gout: he comes away quite stout. *Northanger Abbey*

SMALLRIDGE, MRS.: An acquaintance of Mrs. Elton's sister, who needs a governess in a great hurry and engages Jane Fairfax. Jane is at first adamant against the position, then accepts after breaking her secret engagement with Frank Churchill, then again retracts when the engagement is renewed. Mrs. Smallridge bears no resentment for this vacillation. *Emma*

SMITH: A friend of Mr. Rushworth, whose grounds at Compton have been laid out by the improver, Repton, thus firing his friend with emulation. *Mansfield Park*

SMITH, CHARLES: Marries Anne Elliot's friend, being already an intimate friend of Mr. William Elliot. At first the Smiths live in better style than their friend and often assist him with money, but later when Elliot marries an heiress he leads them into expenses beyond their fortune, then refuses help. A man of warm feelings, easy temper, careless habits and not strong understanding, Smith is led by his friend and probably despised by him. He dies, making Elliot the executor of his will. He leaves only debts to his impoverished invalid widow, as his property in the West Indies, potentially recoverable, is under a sequestration that Elliot refuses to enquire into. *Persuasion*

SMITH, MRS.: Née Hamilton. Three years older than Anne

Elliot, whom she befriends and protects at school. Later their positions are reversed when Anne finds her alone, widowed, impoverished and crippled by rheumatic fever in lodgings in Bath, grateful for her visits. Wretched in circumstances she is still happy in her elasticity of mind, the power of turning readily from evil to good which is not acquired by fortitude or religion but is 'the choicest gift of Heaven'. Anne's cousin, her late husband's close friend, has led him into debt and is now refusing to ameliorate her situation by acting in his affairs, though executor of his will. Silent at first about this, thinking Anne is to marry him, she later reveals his character, warning her against him. Her affairs are unravelled by Captain Wentworth when he marries Anne, but she is not spoilt by good fortune, retaining her natural endowment of good spirits—'She might have been absolutely rich and perfectly healthy, and yet be happy'. *Persuasion*

SMITH, HARRIET: The natural daughter of somebody who places her at Miss Goddard's school. Short, plump, and fair, with a fine bloom, regular features and a look of great sweetness, she is remarkable for her beauty and the sincerity, simplicity and generosity of her nature. She is at first inclined to favour the honest, plebian farmer Robert Martin, but is encouraged by Emma Woodhouse, who befriends her, to fancy the vicar Mr. Elton who is attracted by her beauty. She is unhappy though humble when it appears he really wishes to marry Emma. When snubbed by the resentful Elton at a ball she is rescued by Mr. Knightley, and she becomes attached to him. Continually led on by Emma's over-estimation, she imagines he returns her feelings. Disappointed again, a short visit to Emma's sister in London reconciles her to marrying Robert Martin. The sort of girl who having once begun must always be in love with someone, she is in danger of losing her modest artlessness through Emma's overweening fantasies. She turns out to be the daughter of a respectable tradesman and after her marriage gradually loses touch with Emma. *Emma*

SMITH, MISS: An acquaintance of Mrs. Hughes, who dances with Henry Tilney. *Northanger Abbey*

SMITH, MRS.: An elderly invalid living at Ash Court, a cousin of Willoughby who is dependent on her. He hopes to marry Marianne Dashwood on his expectations from Mrs. Smith, but when she dismisses him from her house and favour, having heard of his seduction of Eliza Williams, he seeks money elsewhere by marrying an heiress. The purity of her life, formality of her notions and ignorance of the world make her implacable against him, if he will not marry Eliza. Later, however, she forgives him on the grounds of his marriage to a woman of character—a bitter irony, as her forgiveness (and her money) would equally therefore have followed his honourable marriage to Marianne. *Sense and Sensibility*

SNEYD: Tom Bertram's friend, who takes him to Ramsgate to meet his family there. *Mansfield Park*

SNEYD, MRS.: Mother of Tom Bertram's friend and of the two Miss Sneyds; she is blamed for causing confusion by making no distinction of dress and manners between the daughter who is 'out' and the one who is not. *Mansfield Park*

SNEYD, MISS: Elder sister of a friend of Tom Bertram who severely offends her by paying attention to her younger sister. *Mansfield Park*

SNEYD, AUGUSTA: Younger sister of a friend of Tom Bertram. She leads him into a *faux pas* by confidently welcoming his conversation and attention which should have been devoted to her elder sister who is already 'out', whereas she is not. *Mansfield Park*

SOPHIA: *see* Emily and Sophia

SPARKS, MISS: An acquaintance of the Miss Steeles. *Sense and Sensibility*

SPEED, MRS.: Usually opens the door of Mrs. Smith's lodgings—perhaps the landlady. *Persuasion*

SPICERS, THE: They have influence with the Bishop that may be used on Charles Hayter's behalf. *Persuasion*

STEELE, ANNE (NANCY): Elder sister of Lucy, a very plain though good-natured woman of nearly thirty. Ignorant and inquisitive, her vulgar freedom and folly are often an embarrassment to her sister, whose secret engagement she unwisely betrays. *Sense and Sensibility*

STEELE, LUCY: A very pretty girl of two or three and twenty, shrewd and self-interested, a niece of Mr. Pratt the tutor at whose house she meets and later becomes secretly engaged to his pupil Edward Ferrars. She holds him to the engagement though she suspects his reluctance and preference for Elinor Dashwood. Staying with her third cousin Lady Middleton, the Dashwood's neighbour, she meets Elinor and warns her off by 'confiding' her secret engagement. In London when Mrs. Ferrars snubs Elinor by pointedly preferring Lucy, her sister presumes unwisely on this and betrays the secret. Still adheres to Edward after he is disinherited for her sake, but skilfully takes the opportunity of his brother Robert's visits to captivate him, and elopes with him. To the end she shows ill-nature by pretending to Elinor's servant that she has married Edward. Though pitiable for the lack of education that spoils her evident intelligence and wit, she is naturally devoid of integrity and delicacy. *Sense and Sensibility*

STEPHEN: A coachman or postilion, steady enough to take Lady Bertram in her coach to Sotherton. *Mansfield Park*

ST. IVES, LORD: Disgusts Sir Walter Elliot by reaching higher rank than him for distinguished service in the navy, though his father is a country curate without bread to eat. *Persuasion*

STOKES, MRS.: Landlady of the Crown Inn, where Mr. Weston's ball is held. *Emma*

STONE, MR.: A 'horrid man' who detains Mr. Gardiner on business on Lydia Bennett's wedding day. *Pride and Prejudice*

STORNAWAY, LORD: Married by Lady Stornaway for his money, but stupid, of ill appearance and character, with not even the air of a gentleman. *Mansfield Park*

STORNAWAY, FLORA, LADY: Née Ross. Originally more the intimate friend of Mary Crawford than her sister Janet, though Flora and Mary have not been close for three years. The first summer she comes out is 'dying' for Henry Crawford. She jilts a very nice young man in the Blues for Lord Stornaway. *Mansfield Park*

SUCKLING, MR.: Brother-in-law of Mrs. Elton who is very proud of him. He lives at Maple Grove and keeps two carriages, one of them a barouche-landau. *Emma*

SUCKLING, MRS. SELINA: Née Hawkins. Mrs. Elton's elder sister, mild to a fault. *Emma*

T

TAYLOR, MISS: *see* Weston, Mrs. Anna

TAYLOR, MRS.: An acquaintance of Mrs. Jennings who tells her of Willoughby's marriage, learning of it from a close friend of his fiancée. *Sense and Sensibility*

THOMAS: The Dashwoods' manservant at their Barton cottage. He meets Lucy Steele just after her marriage to Robert Ferrars, and is purposely deceived by her into reporting that she has married Edward Ferrars. *Sense and Sensibility*

THORPE, MRS.: A former schoolfellow of Mrs. Allen, meets her again in Bath, unexpectedly but fortunately as the Allens know no one there. A lawyer's widow and not a very rich one, she is a gentle, good-humoured, well-meaning woman, and a very indulgent mother. *Northanger Abbey*

THORPE, ANNE: One of Mrs. Thorpe's daughters, not as handsome as Isabella though pretending to be. Her brother John will not drive her to Clifton because she has thick ankles, but she consoles herself with her new friends Emily and Sophia. *Northanger Abbey*

THORPE, EDWARD: One of Mrs. Thorpe's sons, at Merchant Taylors'. *Northanger Abbey*

THORPE, ISABELLA: Mrs. Thorpe's eldest daughter, has considerable personal beauty, but is shallow, artificial, affected and selfish. She becomes Catherine Morland's friend and introduces her to Gothic horror novels, the absurdity, inconsistency and indiscriminate emotion of which suit her very well. After her engagement to Catherine's brother James Morland, learning that his father's income is less than she thinks, she encourages Captain Tilney's attentions and breaks off the engagement, but being disappointed by him, tries (in vain) to reconcile herself to James through Catherine. Her affection for both James and Catherine is as empty as its expression is excessive. *Northanger Abbey*

THORPE, JOHN: Mrs. Thorpe's son, a stout young man of middling height 'who, with a plain face and ungraceful form, seemed fearful of being too handsome unless he wore the dress of a groom, and too much like a gentleman unless he were easy where he ought to be civil, and impudent where he might be allowed to be easy'. His own attentions to Catherine, sister of his friend James Morland, cause him to boast falsely of her wealth and expectations to General Tilney, a misunderstanding that later has ill consequences: when Catherine rejects his first advances and his sister Isabella jilts James, he is so annoyed he not only denies her fictional wealth but describes her family as poorer and needier than they are; and this infuriates the General against the innocent Catherine. As inconsistent and superficial as his sister Isabella, he is also more directly boastful and more boring. *Northanger Abbey*

THORPE, MARIA: Sister of Isabella Thorpe, a smart girl though not beautiful. *Northanger Abbey*

THORPE, WILLIAM: One of Mrs. Thorpe's sons, a sailor. *Northanger Abbey*

TILNEY, GENERAL: A man of fine appearance and considerable wealth, he owns Northanger Abbey, and is the father of Frederick, Henry and Eleanor. Proud, narrow-minded and worldly, he is accustomed to give law in his family and peremptorily demands submission to his whims. While staying at Bath, he is misled by John Thorpe into believing Henry's acquaintance, Catherine Morland, to be a great heiress, encourages this acquaintance, and invites her to Northanger. There Catherine, influenced by sensational novels, imagines he has murdered or imprisoned his late wife. When this fantasy is dispelled, he is disillusioned again by Thorpe about Catherine's wealth and, furious, vents his disappointment by ordering that she leave the house as soon as possible. Ordering Henry to think of her no more, he is amazed to find his autocracy opposed, and parts from his son in anger. The good humour aroused by Eleanor's marriage to a rich Viscount however provides the opportunity for obtaining his consent. Arbitrary, wilful and short-tempered, his inhibiting influence is felt even when he is being most attentively gallant, and Catherine feels his worldly, selfish discourtesy is hardly less reprehensible than her early imaginings of murder and cruelty. *Northanger Abbey*

TILNEY, MRS.: Née Drummond. Dies nine years before the novel begins; Catherine Morland imagines her murdered or imprisoned by her husband. *Northanger Abbey*

TILNEY, ELEANOR: General Tilney's daughter, whose sweet, quiet character is not valued by him. On a visit to Bath with her father and brother Henry she meets Catherine Morland, soon sees she is in love with Henry, and becomes her friend. Instructed by her father, she invites her to stay at her home Northanger Abbey, where her brother's absences have left her often solitary since her mother's death. Improving in intimacy and agreeing in occupation with Catherine, she is ashamed and dismayed to give her father's commands that Catherine must leave their house as soon as possible, without escort or courtesy—she has to lend her the money for the journey. She has an admirer, whom she prefers, and who, unexpectedly succeeding to title and fortune, is able to marry her, and gratifying her father's pride by bringing a viscount into the family, she persuades him to allow Henry to marry Catherine. Happy in her marriage, there is 'no one more entitled by unpretending merit, or better prepared by habitual suffering to receive and enjoy felicity'. *Northanger Abbey*

TILNEY, CAPTAIN FREDERICK: Elder son and heir of General Tilney, a very fashionable-looking handsome young man. From vanity he flatters and flirts with Isabella Thorpe, knowing her to be engaged to James Morland, then having tempted her to break her engagement, he withdraws his attention and departs. *Northanger Abbey*

TILNEY, HENRY: Younger son of General Tilney, a clergyman, of four or five and twenty, rather tall with a pleasing countenance and a very intelligent and lively eye, and if not handsome is very near it. While visiting Bath with his father and sister, meets Catherine Morland who later stays with them at their home, Northanger Abbey. He laughs at her predilection for horror novels, but is kind and sympathetic when this leads her into embarrassing error. When his father, at first planning his marriage on the mistaken belief that she is an heiress, is disillusioned and discourteously sends her home, Henry is indignant and angry, for though noticing her first partiality for him, affection has followed gratitude and he is sincerely attached to her. Defying his furious, domineering father, he hurries to her home and asks for the heart 'which, perhaps, they pretty equally knew was already entirely his own'. Though his feelings on his vocation and his brother's morals remain unclear, he is a man of more conviction and honour than appears in his usual ironical manner. *Northanger Abbey*

TOM: One of the Westons' servants. *Emma*

TRENT, GOVERNOR: A former inhabitant of Monksford. *Persuasion*

TUPMANS, THE: A family settled at West Hall for eighteen months, coming from Birmingham, expect to be on a footing with Mr. Suckling who has owned nearby Maple Grove for a full eleven years. *Emma*

TURNER'S: A naval shop in Portsmouth. *Mansfield Park*

V

VISCOUNT, THE: The most charming young man in the world who, while still an impoverished commoner, leaves in a drawer the laundry bills that the over-imaginative Catherine Morland expects to be a sensational manuscript. He admires Eleanor Tilney for some time until unexpectedly succeeding to title and fortune, he is able to marry her, and is really deserving of her. *Northanger Abbey*

W

WALKER, MISS: An acquaintance of Mrs. Jennings' friend Mrs. Taylor, hints to her of disagreements between the Ellisons and their ward Sophia Grey, who marries Willoughby. *Sense and Sensibility*

WALLIS, COLONEL: A friend of Mr. Elliot who warns him of Mrs. Clay's evident designs on Sir Walter Elliot. He is introduced by him to Sir Walter, who approves him as a fine-looking man (though sandy-haired). He tells his pretty wife things he had better not. *Persuasion*

WALLIS, MRS.: Wife of Colonel Wallis, she is just giving birth to a baby. Reputed to be both charming and beautiful, though to her nurse, Mrs. Rooke, merely a 'silly, expensive fashionable woman'. *Persuasion*

WALLIS, MRS.: The baker's wife of Highbury, bakes the Bates' apples in her bakery oven. She is said to be capable of incivility and rude answers, but is always very attentive to the impoverished Bates'. *Emma*

WALSH, CAPTAIN: A friend of Mr. Price. *Mansfield Park*

WEBBS, THE MISS: Acquaintances of Lady Catherine de Bourgh. All learn the piano although their father's income is not so good as the Bennetts, who do *not* all learn the piano. *Pride and Prejudice*

WENTWORTH, EDWARD: Brother of Captain Wentworth who stays with him when he has the curacy of Monksford for two or three years; he later moves out of the county, marries and has a parish in Shropshire. *Persuasion*

WENTWORTH, CAPTAIN FREDERICK: When staying with his brother Edward, the curate of Monksford, he falls in love with Anne Elliot, second daughter of Sir Walter. They become engaged although he has no fortune or secure prospects, and she is persuaded, partly for his sake, to break the engagement: he leaves, angry and resentful. His genius and ardour contribute to his good fortune, and he soon distinguishes himself and becomes rich. Eight years later when his sister Mrs. Croft and her husband rent the house that Anne's father can no longer afford to live in, he returns to the district, still resentful, and ready to marry any sweet-tempered pretty woman, provided she has a stronger will than Anne's. Flirting with Henrietta and Louisa Musgrove, his admiration of Louisa's firmness is shaken when that firmness turns into unreasonable obstinacy and precipitates the accident in which she injures her head; Anne's greater rationality and prompt competence are obviously wiser. Thankful for Louisa's recovery, he is appalled to find he has raised expectations that he will marry her, just as he realises her inferiority. He visits his brother to avoid her, and luckily she falls in love with his friend Benwick, so he is free to follow Anne to Bath, where he finds her courted by her eligible cousin William Elliot. His appeal by letter reveals that she still loves him and they marry. It is throughout his open, spontaneous frankness that appeals to Anne, and the risk of impulsiveness and rashness are far preferable to the selfish calculation of the polished man of the world, Mr. Elliot. *Persuasion*

WESTON, MR.: A man of unexceptionable character, easy fortune and pleasant manners, a native of Highbury whose family has for three generations been rising into gentility and property. As a captain in the militia he marries Miss Churchill of a great Yorkshire family, an unsuitable connection which does not produce much happiness, thanks to her unreasonable regrets, and when after three years she dies, their son Frank is adopted by her relations. Then, re-establishing his fortune by trade, he becomes rich enough after twenty years to buy Randalls, a small estate, and marry Emma Woodhouse's amiable but penniless companion Miss Taylor. His warm heart, sweet temper and sociability make him rather too tolerant and undiscriminating. Emma feels that 'to be the favourite and intimate of a man who had so many intimates and confidantes was not the very first distinction in the scale of vanity'. *Emma*

WESTON, MRS. (THE FIRST): Born Miss Churchill of Enscombe of a great Yorkshire family, she falls in love with Mr. Weston, and marries him against her family's wishes. Though she has one sort of spirit she has not the best and in spite of her husband's sweet nature she regrets unreasonably the loss of her great position. Living beyond their means because of her habits of luxury, she dies after three years, leaving her husband rather poorer than before. They have one son (*see* Churchill, Frank). *Emma*

WESTON, MRS. ANNA: As Miss Taylor she is governess to Isabella and Emma Woodhouse, becoming Emma's companion and friend as she grows up. Almost a mother to her for sixteen years, until her marriage to Mr. Weston, she is sadly missed by the Woodhouses; her marriage and departure give Emma the inspiration and leisure for her later disastrous matchmaking. She has never imposed on Emma enough restraint to curb her self-esteem; intelligent, well-informed, useful, gentle, she is 'very fit for a wife, but not at all for a governess'. Has a daughter, Anna. *Emma*

WESTON, FRANK: *see* Churchill, Frank

WESTONS, THE: They visit the Palmers. *Sense and Sensibility*

WHITAKER, MRS.: Mr. Rushworth's housekeeper, who turns away housemaids for wearing white gowns;

a 'treasure', approved by Mrs. Norris, she tells her all about the cows and gives her pheasants' eggs and a cream cheese. *Mansfield Park*

WHITAKERS, THE: A family living near Sir John Middleton, invited to dine and perhaps dance at his home. *Sense and Sensibility*

WICKHAM, OLD MR.: Formerly an attorney, he becomes steward of all the late Mr. Darcy's estates and serves faithfully and well. He has an extravagant wife, which means he would be unable to give his son George a gentleman's education without the assistance of his employer. *Pride and Prejudice*

WICKHAM, MR. GEORGE: Son of a steward at Pemberley, where the owner, the late Mr. Darcy, his godfather and patron, supports him at Cambridge and destines him for the Church. However, his viciousness and want of principle are known to young Mr. Darcy, who later agrees to pay him three thousand pounds in place of the assistance and patronage his godfather intended in the religious vocation he is not fitted for. He pretends to study law, though really living in idleness and vice, and three years later asks for Darcy's financial patronage. Resentful when this is refused, he secretly persuades Darcy's 15-year-old sister to elope with him, partly in revenge, partly for her large fortune, but she confesses the plan to her brother. Later he enters the militia quartered at Meryton where he meets the Bennett sisters, and is particularly attracted to Elizabeth, but wishes to marry the plain Miss King when she inherits money. He blackens Darcy's character in the neighbourhood, and is a general favourite, until his departure leaving debts everywhere. He elopes with Lydia Bennett, but, still hoping for an heiress, has to be bribed to marry her by Darcy. His affection soon sinks into indifference, and they manage badly, always spending more than they ought. He owes his conquests to his very handsome face and winningly soft manners, and many, like Elizabeth, let his appearance vouch for his morals: later, however, she seeks in vain for evidence of real goodness under the surface. *Pride and Prejudice*

WILCOX: The Bertrams' coachman, his convenience is always particularly considered by Mrs. Norris (thus inconveniencing everyone else). He complains bitterly of the narrow road to Sotherton scratching the carriage, being (according to Maria) 'a stupid old fellow who does not know how to drive'. *Sense and Sensibility*

WILLIAM: The Tilneys' servant in Bath: Catherine Morland is in such haste to speak to the Tilneys that she hurries by him, arousing General Tilney's anger that William has not announced her, until she explains. *Northanger Abbey*

WILLIAMS, MISS ELIZA: Illegitimate daughter of Eliza Brandon, Colonel Brandon's sister-in-law and childhood sweetheart, taken in by him as a child when her mother dies of consumption in a debtors' prison. Placed at school until she is fourteen, she then lives with a respectable woman in Dorsetshire, but while visiting a friend in Bath she disappears, seduced by Willoughby. Later a letter to her guardian discloses that she is abandoned, in want, and expecting a child. Colonel Brandon removes her and her child to the country, and fights a duel with her seducer. Willoughby later blames her for her violent passions and weak understanding. *Sense and Sensibility*

WILLOUGHBY, JOHN: A very handsome young man of five and twenty, owner of Combe Magna, a pretty little estate in Somerset, though his extravagance and mounting debts make him dependent on his rich old cousin Mrs. Smith. In Bath he meets, seduces and abandons Eliza Williams, whose guardian Colonel Brandon later fights a duel with him. Falls in love with Marianne Dashwood, but while he hesitates to propose to her, Mrs. Smith hears of Eliza's plight and dismisses him from her favour, making it necessary for him to save his fortune by becoming engaged to the heiress Sophia Grey, whom he knows is ready to have him. When Marianne unknowingly accosts him at a party, he snubs her, and writes a letter dictated by the jealous Miss Grey disclaiming their acquaintance. Later, hearing of Marianne's serious illness, he goes to explain himself to her sister Elinor, and excuse at least his earlier conduct as sincere. His repentance is lasting though he survives 'to exert and frequently to enjoy himself'. Of good abilities, open and affectionate manners, he has a natural ardour of mind very like Marianne's, but more confirmed in self-indulgence, his ardour is not directed by reason or principle. *Sense and Sensibility*

WILLOUGHBY, MRS.: *see* Grey, Miss Sophia

WINGFIELD, MR.: Isabella Knightley's apothecary and medical adviser in London, on whom she relies as much as her father relies on Mr. Perry. *Emma*

WOODHOUSE, EMMA: Handsome, clever and rich, with a comfortable home and a happy disposition, she lives nearly twenty-one years with very little to distress or vex her. She is brought up by her friend and governess Mrs. Weston (Miss Taylor), and is the mistress of her valetudinarian father's house, Hartfield. Distress and vexation arise, however, from her matchmaking efforts on behalf of her new friend Harriet Smith, whose innocent, ignorant flattery confirms her own self-esteem. First assuming the pretty, illegitimate Harriet has attracted the young vicar Mr. Elton (who in fact aspires to Emma herself), she persuades Harriet to refuse her worthy but plebeian farmer suitor, Robert Martin. Finding her mistake, she more cautiously matches the handsome Frank Churchill to Harriet, quelling her own passing attraction to him, only to hear he is secretly engaged to Jane Fairfax, and is even more appalled to hear Harriet herself has hopes of Mr. Knightley, her lifelong friend, whom she now realises she loves. Her humiliation is increased because she has indiscreetly joked about Jane to Frank, not knowing their relationship, and has been reprimanded by Mr. Knightley for an unkind criticism of Jane's garrulous aunt Miss Bates. However, she is reprieved by learning of Mr. Knightley's love for her and consoled by Harriet's own speedy consolation by her farmer suitor. All her errors spring from her illusions about other peoples' characters and motives, and about her own powers—her penetration being less than she thinks, and she finally learns to live less in her imagination. *Emma*

WOODHOUSE, MR. HENRY: An elderly valetudinarian, wealthy owner of Hartfield, father of Isabella and Emma. Much older in ways than in years, though everywhere beloved for the friendliness of his heart and his amiable temper, his talents could not have recommended him at any time. Frequently his punctilious kindliness is at war with his invalid caution; he is always uncertain whether to give or withhold rich indigestible refreshments for his guests. His dislike of all kinds of novelty and change, including marriage, is a difficulty when Emma wishes to marry Mr. Knightley, solved by their both remaining at Hartfield with him. *Emma*

WRIGHT: The housekeeper at the vicarage; also does Mrs. Elton's hair for Mr. Weston's ball. *Emma*

Y

YATES, THE HON. JOHN: A new intimate friend of Tom Bertram, with not much to recommend him beyond habits of fashion and expense and being the younger son of a lord. Coming from a houseparty where amateur theatricals have been interrupted, he inspires most of the younger people at Mansfield Park to perform a play. He tries to make himself agreeable to Tom's younger sister Julia, without success, while she is suffering from jealousy of Henry Crawford. To his amazement he is balked again of his play by the return of the disapproving Sir Thomas. Later he pays attentions to Julia in London, which she ignores until her sister's elopement makes her anxious to escape her father's severity at all costs and she elopes with him. Afterwards he is desirous of being properly received into the family, defers to Sir Thomas, proves to have a better income than was expected, and shows signs of becoming less trifling. *Mansfield Park*

YOUNGE, MRS.: Lives with Miss Darcy as her companion in London, and visits Ramsgate with her, where they are followed by her acquaintance Mr. Wickham. Suspected of collusion in Wickham's planned elopement with her charge, she is dismissed and takes a large house in London, where she lives by letting lodgings. Later she has to be bribed to reveal where Wickham and Lydia Bennett are staying. *Pride and Prejudice*

Who's Who in the Brontës

A

A——, M.: A French Academician, dines with **Mr. Home** de Bassompierre. *Villette*

AGNES: Bad-tempered Flemish servant of Mme. Walravens. *Villette*

AIGREDOUX, MME.: Paulina Home's former schoolmistress, who could not cope with Mr. Home's constant presence in her school. *Villette*

AINSLEY, MARY ANN: An old maid of fifty, *very* ugly. Completely unselfish, toils for others, usually unappreciated. Her life is Christ-like, and she perseveres without needing any earthly reward: Caroline Helstone, trying to follow her example, finds this too hard. *Shirley*

ANGELIQUE: A titled pupil of Mme. Beck; sits with Blanche de Melcy. *Villette*

ARCHER, DAME: The woman who first shows the new born Hareton Earnshaw to his father—probably a midwife. *Wuthering Heights*

ARMITAGE, MR.: A mill-owner. In spite of conciliating his workers, is shot at when wages and work decrease. *Shirley*

ARMITAGE, THE MISSES: The six daughters of the mill-owner Mr. Armitage. Robert Moore's name linked with the red-haired one. *Shirley*

ASHBY, SIR THOMAS: Owner of Ashby Park, who has a pale face though blotchy and disagreeably red about the eyelids, plain features and a general appearance of langour and flatness, relieved by a sinister expression about the mouth, and dull soulless eyes. Has been very dissolute, but Rosalie Murray marries him for his title and property. He objects to her flirtation and extravagance in London and takes her to Ashby Park. Is disappointed to have only a daughter. *Agnes Grey*

ASHBY, LADY: *see* Murray, Rosalie

ASHBY, LADY (THE ELDER): Mother of Sir Thomas, a sour, taciturn old lady, blindly attached to her dissolute son. Her daughter-in-law refuses her offer to move out of Ashby Park (a refusal later regretted). Criticises and over-rules Rosalie, who hates her, but Agnes Grey has heard good as well as evil of her, and suggests her affection and support could be won. *Agnes Grey*

B

BARBARA: A servant at Lowood School, waits on Miss Temple. *Jane Eyre*

BARRACLOUGH, MOSES: A 'joined Methodist' and thorough hypocrite. In spite of his wooden leg, his preaching attracts large congregations of weaver girls. A leader of the machine breakers, he later heads a deputation asking Robert Moore to leave the country, whereupon Moore has him arrested. Is sentenced to transportation. *Shirley*

BARRETT, MRS.: A housekeeper, once Lucy's nurse. A grave, judicious woman, she informs Lucy of possibilities of teaching English abroad. *Villette*

BASSOMPIERRE, DE: *see* Home de Bassompierre

BATES, MR.: The surgeon who treats the pupils of Lowood School. *Jane Eyre*

BECK, MARIE MODESTE: Née Kint. Mistress of a boarding school in the Rue Fossette. On M. Paul's recommendation she hires Lucy Snowe without references when she arrives penniless and friendless on her doorstep, and later promotes her from nursery governess to English teacher. A materialist, she stands in contrast to the more spiritual Lucy throughout the novel, especially as a would-be rival for the attentions of the two heroes, Dr. John and her cousin M. Paul Emanuel. At first, her cool, enlightened self-interest is welcome, but as Lucy's emotional torments grow, Mme. Beck's rationality is twisted by jealousy and she becomes actively malignant in separating Lucy from M. Paul. In league with his confessor Père Silas she prevails on him to visit family estates abroad; he is probably drowned on the return voyage.

A 'compact little pony' in appearance, she hides under her affability the character of a domestic Napoleon, controlling her establishment through faultless organisation and systematic espionage. In keeping with the ironic Human Justice of this novel, she 'prospered all the days of her life'. *Villette*

BECK, DESIREE: Mme. Beck's eldest child, sly, dishonest and destructive. Her bad tendencies are exacerbated by the Continental education system of 'surveillance' (spying) instead of being checked by wholesome British moral teaching and trust. *Villette*

BECK, FIFINE: Mme. Beck's second child, an honest gleeful little soul (resembles her dead father). Her broken arm is the cause of Dr. John Bretton's first summons to the school. *Villette*

BECK, GEORGETTE: Mme. Beck's youngest child, sensitive and loving, affectionate to Lucy. *Villette*

BENSON: The Huntingdon's butler. Often insulted by Arthur Huntingdon, he helps Arthur's wife to escape secretly from her husband. *The Tenant of Wildfell Hall*

BIRTWHISTLE FAMILY, THE: Attend the Whitsuntide gathering. *Shirley*

BLEMONT, CAROLINE DE: Pupil at Mlle. Reuter's school, sits in the front row. Of noble family, very dark and beautiful, she is already devoid of morals, as notoriously is her mother. *The Professor*

BLIGH, MR.: Mr. Weston's predecessor as Mr. Hatfield's curate at Horton, a 'seedy old fellow' who gets a long-wished-for living elsewhere. *Agnes Grey*

BLOOMFIELD, MR.: Husband of Mrs. Bloomfield, a rather thin, ungentlemanly, trivial-minded man whose dingy complexion and waspish temper Agnes attributes to excess gin and water. Quarrels with his wife publicly over her housekeeping and reprimands Agnes by talking *at* her about the children's unruliness. *Agnes Grey*

BLOOMFIELD, MRS.: A tall, spare, stately woman, sallow and black-haired, Agnes Grey's first employer. Chilly in manner, blind to her children's faults, she forbids most punishments by Agnes and countermands her other sanctions, dismissing her within a year for failing to influence her charges. *Agnes Grey*

BLOOMFIELD, FANNY: Four years old, a mischievous, intractable little creature, given up to falsehood and deception. Her two weapons are 'spitting in the faces of those who incur her displeasure and bellowing like a bull when her unreasonable desires were not gratified'. *Agnes Grey*

BLOOMFIELD, HARRIET: A little, broad, fat, merry, playful thing of scarcely two, with whom Agnes Grey has nothing to do. *Agnes Grey*

BLOOMFIELD, MARY ANN: Eldest daughter of the Bloomfields, nearly six, an affected, conceited child who prefers rolling on the floor to any other amusement. Given to tantrums, stupid and obstinate. *Agnes Grey*

BLOOMFIELD, TOM: Seven-year-old son of the Bloomfields, who not only refuses to be ruled by the governess Agnes Grey but wishes to rule her. Self-important and defiant, his idea of enjoyment is torturing live fledglings. *Agnes Grey*

BOARHAM, MR.: A friend of Helen Huntingdon's aunt, a dreadful bore who courts Helen, and though decent enough talks incessantly and is not discouraged even by outright refusal of his proposal. *The Tenant of Wildfell Hall*

BOISSEC and ROCHEMORT: Dandified professors, one dark, one light, from Paul Emanuel's college. They suggest Lucy's essays are plagiarism and impose an impromptu examination on her. A pair of cold-blooded fops and pedants, sceptics and scoffers, they inspire her to write on the kind of 'Human Justice' (partial and cruel) that her life shows her. *Villette*

BOOTH, OLD JAMES: Gardener at Fieldhead, Shirley Keeldar's house. *Shirley*

BOULTBY, DR. THOMAS: Rector of Whinbury. A stubborn old Welshman, hot, opinionated and obstinate, does much good though not by stealth. *Shirley*

BOULTBY, MRS.: Wife of Dr. Boultby, his deferential admirer. *Shirley*

BOULTBY, GRACE: May be Mrs. Boultby's name, may be her daughter. *Shirley*

BRANDERHAM, THE REV. JABES: Author of a sermon on 'Seventy Times Seven and the First of the Seventy-First' delivered in Gimmerton Chapel near Wuthering Heights. A printed copy of it contains some of Catherine Earnshaw's journal, read by Lockwood who then dreams he listens to the endless sermon, is reprimanded by Branderham and then attacked by the congregation. *Wuthering Heights*

BRAUN, ANNA: A worthy, hearty woman of forty-five, gives German lessons to Lucy Snowe and Paulina Home; is amazed both by their British reserve and their British application. *Villette*

BRETTON, DR.: Mrs. Bretton's husband, John Graham's father, a physician. Dies before the novel starts. *Villette*

BRETTON, DR. JOHN GRAHAM: Only after long delay is handsome young Dr. John who attends Mme. Beck's pupils revealed as the Graham Bretton, son of Lucy Snowe's godmother, who previously appears as a youth. At first infatuated with Ginevra Fanshawe, he later marries Paulina Home. A deceptively complex character, who has some attractions for Lucy, he is responsive but difficult to influence: '*impressionable* he was as dimpling water, but, almost as water, unimpressible.' Neither tempered by suffering like Lucy, nor complacent like Ginevra, he is 'a man of luck, a man of success': in an all too imperfect world, his robust earthly happiness is 'the attesting trace and lingering evidence of Eden'. *Villette*

BRETTON, MRS. LOUISA: Mother of John Graham Bretton. It is in her house at Bretton that we first meet her god-daughter, Lucy Snowe; and the child Paulina Mary Home at the same time meets John Graham whom she later marries. A sensible, robust, unsentimental woman, she is admired by Lucy, but, for all her kindness and shrewdness, she is unaware of both the imaginative and the neurotic aspects of Lucy's nature. As Lucy grows up, both she and the Brettons have financial misfortunes and lose touch: the Brettons unlike Lucy survive unchanged largely because of their physical and mental vigour. When her son makes good as a doctor in Villette, Mrs. Bretton joins him there and recreates the original Bretton home at *La*

Terrasse: here Lucy is carried when taken ill during the summer vacation. Though a devoted mother, she is not as possessive as Mr. Home. Prosperous as the novel closes, she will die in 'ripe old age'. *Villette*

BRIGGS: A solicitor of London. Accompanies Mason to interrupt Rochester's wedding to Jane Eyre which he does by declaring a 'just cause or impediment': the existence of a living wife. He is acting for Jane's uncle who is dying in the West Indies. *Jane Eyre*

BROADBENT, DR.: A beautiful speaker at a Bible Society meeting, such a dear, good, useful man—'only like a butcher in appearance'. *Shirley*

BROC, MARIE: A cretin pupil at Mme. Beck's school. She is left at the school during part of the long summer vacation and Lucy Snowe, who likewise has nowhere else to go, has to care for her. The cretin, with her mindless, exhausting demands, both provokes and personifies the first stage of Lucy's mental breakdown, where the physical routine becomes intolerable, devoid of occupation and companionship. *Villette*

BROCKLEHURST, AUGUSTA: Mr. Brocklehurst's second daughter, visits Lowood school and comments on the poverty of the girls and their evident amazement at her own fine clothes. *Jane Eyre*

BROCKLEHURST, MASTER BROUGHTON: Youngest child of Mr. Brocklehurst. He may be the paragon who says he prefers learning psalms to ginger nuts and daily receives twice as many ginger nuts as recompense for his infant piety. *Jane Eyre*

BROCKLEHURST, NAOMI: Commemorated in a stone inscription over the door of Lowood school, part of which she had rebuilt. Mother of Mr. Brocklehurst, treasurer of the school. *Jane Eyre*

BROCKLEHURST, MR. ROBERT: Clergyman and treasurer of the semi-charity school Lowood. Appears to the little Jane Eyre as a 'black column', his grim face embellished with bushy brows, inquisitive grey eyes, a great nose and large prominent teeth. Told by Mrs. Reed that Jane is deceitful, he relays this judgment to the assembled school when she arrives. As an administrator he stints the pupils in clothing and food in the name of humility and fortitude (in startling contrast to the luxurious upbringing of his own family) thus predisposing the girls to an epidemic of typhus. This is investigated, and his control limited and supervised. *Jane Eyre*

BROCKLEHURST, MRS.: Wife of Mr. Brocklehurst. Is not included in the policy of economy and humility he imposes on Lowood school, which she visits in elaborate and expensive gowns. With her daughters she rummages through the housekeeping and washing arrangements at the school and reprimands the teachers. *Jane Eyre*

BROCKLEHURST, MISS: A fine girl of seventeen, Mr. Brocklehurst's eldest daughter, she visits Lowood school where her expensive, fashionable clothes contrast with the plainness imposed by her father on the schoolgirls. *Jane Eyre*

BROCKLEHURST, THEODORE: Third child of Mr. Brocklehurst. *Jane Eyre*

BROWN, MR.: An elderly gentleman, very grave, business-like and respectable-looking, living in Brussels, to whom Hunsden gives William Crimsworth a letter of introduction. He finds him a post at M. Pelet's school as 'Professor' of English and Latin. Relays Brussels gossip to Hunsden, especially about Mlle. Reuter and Crimsworth, for which the latter calls him 'an old woman'. *The Professor*

BROWN: Servant of the Murrays, a mincing damsel. *Agnes Grey*

BROWN, SMITH, NICHOLL, ECCLES: Acquaintances of William Crimsworth while he works for his brother, negatively mentioned as affording him no pleasure by their company. *The Professor*

BROWNE, NANCY: An old widow of Horton whose inflammation of the eyes and rheumatism make her grateful when Agnes Grey visits and reads to her. When afflicted by religious melancholy she is scolded peremptorily by the vicar, Mr. Hatfield, for idle fancifulness, but Mr. Weston the curate shows his better nature by patiently calming her fears. Also, BILL, her son, a farm labourer. *Agnes Grey*

BURNS, HELEN: Pupil at Lowood school, thirteen years old, neglected by her father who has remarried. Though intelligent and reflective, she is untidy and absent-minded, so that she is victimised by one of the teachers. She befriends the young Jane Eyre, whose passionate, resentful feelings she seeks to temper with her own creed of mildness and submissiveness. Already consumptive, she dies of tuberculosis during the typhus epidemic. Although she appears only briefly, her stoical, spiritual philosophy has a lasting effect on Jane's personality. *Jane Eyre*

C

CANDACE: The little Paulina Home's doll, so called after the Ethiopian queens because of its 'begrimed complexion'. *Villette*

CAROLINE: The fiancée Lord Lowborough loves and loses by losing his fortune. *The Tenant of Wildfell Hall*

CARTER, MR.: A surgeon, admitted into Rochester's confidence about the identity of the madwoman (Rochester's wife) kept secretly at Thornfield, whom he sometimes has to attend—also her victims, such as her brother Mason. Later he has to amputate Rochester's right arm, injured when Thornfield burns down. *Jane Eyre*

CATHERINE ———, LADY: A young Irish baroness, attends the school of Frances Crimsworth (née Henri) in Brussels, and is dearly loved by her for her enthusiastic heart, clever head, generosity and genius. *The Professor*

CAVE, MARY: A statuesque, silent beauty, once loved by Mr. Yorke, marries Mr. Helstone. Dies after five years of marriage. Rumours of neglect and ill-treatment motivate Yorke's hostility to Helstone. *Shirley*

CHARLES: A schoolfriend of William Crimsworth, he is a sarcastic, shrewd, observant, cold-blooded creature, to whom William writes an account of his early life (this letter forming the first chapter of the novel) and is then abandoned. He never receives the letter, having accepted a government appointment in the colonies, thus passing from our ken. *The Professor*

CHARLES: Lucy Snowe's uncle, whom she is said to resemble. *Villette*

CHARLOTTE: A younger sister of the channel ferry stewardess, about to marry imprudently. *Villette*

CHOLMONDELY, MRS.: A gay, fashionable lady living in Villette, who acts as Ginevra's chaperon in society. *Villette*

CLARA: A German girl, successor to Céline Varens and Giacinta as Mr. Rochester's third mistress. Singularly handsome, honest and quiet, but heavy, mindless and unimpressible, so that he is glad to set her up in a good line of business and so get decently rid of her. His sense of degradation in hiring even an honest mistress serves as warning to Jane Eyre. *Jane Eyre*

CORALIE: A pupil of Madame Beck. *Villette*

CRIMSWORTH, MR.: An astute, mercantile man, uncle of Edward and William. Brings up the latter until he is nine, then blackmails the noble Seacombes, who are contesting a doubtful Parliamentary seat, into paying for their nephew's education at Eton. *The Professor*

CRIMSWORTH, EDWARD: William's brother, ten years his senior, entirely brought up by a paternal uncle and a successful manufacturer. A very handsome man, he marries a rich mill-owner's daughter. Employs William as a clerk, develops an instinctive antipathy for him, bullies him, and finally suspecting him of raising public opinion by complaints (in fact, the accusations stem from Yorke Hunsden) tries to drive him out with a whip. Later is said to have gone bankrupt and ill-treated his wife, who leaves him; later still makes a new fortune by railway speculation. *The Professor*

CRIMSWORTH, MRS.: Wife of Edward and daughter of a rich mill-owner. Young, tall, well-shaped, but red-haired and materialistic. Later, ill-treated by her husband, returns to her father. *The Professor*

CRIMSWORTH, VICTOR: Son of William Crimsworth and Frances, he becomes a serious but ardent boy, due to be sent to Eton for hardening off, after his mother's sympathetic understanding and Hunsden's intellectual provocation. *The Professor*

CRIMSWORTH, WILLIAM: Known as 'the Professor'. Younger son of a failed manufacturer and an aristocratic lady, who dies at his birth. He is brought up first by a paternal uncle, then his noble relatives (under pressure) pay for his education at Eton. Having offended them by declining to enter the Church, he enters his elder brother Edward's business as a clerk. Alienated by Edward's increasing hostility, he goes to Belgium, and becomes English teacher (professor) in M. Pelet's boys' school. Engaged also to give additional lessons in the girls' school next door, he is at first attracted then disillusioned by the headmistress, Mlle. Zoraïde Reuter, who is secretly engaged to Pelet. Her infatuation with Crimsworth grows as his wanes, and jealously she dismisses the Anglo-Swiss needlework teacher, Frances Henri, whom he obviously admires. Angry, he resigns from the school, and when she is reunited in marriage with Pelet, resigns also his other post, not trusting her morals nor indeed his own in too great proximity. Thus destitute just as he is beginning to think of marrying Frances, he is after an anxious period given a much better paid position in a big school, on the recommendation of a businessman whose son he has saved from drowning. He marries Frances and they become rich enough to retire to England with their young son Victor. Plain, shortsighted and unsociable, Crimsworth never goes to extremes: he can renounce money on a matter of principle, but generally keeps a careful eye on his finances and sees his renunciation as a duty not a martyrdom: 'the man of regular life and rational mind never despairs.' Cool to the point of pedantry, he is evidently an ideal 'professor'. *The Professor*

D

D, MRS.: Headmistress of the best English girls' school in Brussels. Employs Frances Henri as a French teacher on Mrs. Watson's recommendation. *The Professor*

DAVIES, MR.: Married to Ginevra's sister, he is much older than her father and marked by yellow fever, 'but then he is rich'. *Villette*

DAVIES, AUGUSTA, née FANSHAWE: Ginevra's elder sister, beautiful and dark, married to the old but rich Mr. Davies and considered to have 'done perfectly well'. *Villette*

DEAN, ELLEN (NELLY): Called 'Mrs.', though unmarried, housekeeper at Thrushcross Grange where she tells the tenant Lockwood the history of Wuthering Heights, ancient home of the Earnshaws. Daughter of Hindley Earnshaw's nurse, she is companion to Hindley and his sister Catherine, later becoming nurse of his son Hareton, whom she has to leave when she moves to Thrushcross Grange because the wayward, demanding Catherine, who marries its owner Edgar Linton, is so strongly attached to her. Uncertain whether to condone or condemn Catherine's visits from Heathcliff, she eventually tells Edgar of them and of his designs on Isabella Linton, treats Catherine's rage as insincere, and is blamed for her subsequent fever. When Catherine dies in childbirth, nurses her daughter Cathy but later is unable to prevent Heathcliff's plans to marry her charge to his weak, malicious son. After Cathy's forced marriage and Edgar's death, she remains at Thrushcross Grange, forbidden to visit Wuthering Heights until Heathcliff's obsession with visions of the dead Catherine makes him invite her back as housekeeper, where she stays until his death and the marriage of the now widowed Cathy and Hareton. A responsible, well-informed woman, she has a strong attachment for the Earnshaws, the Lintons and even Heathcliff, and while her morality and common sense is always opposed to their wild loves and hates, she recognises the force of their passions. *Wuthering Heights*

DEB: Mr. Yorke's Servant. *Shirley*

DENT, COLONEL: A fine, soldierly man, one of Rochester's houseparty at Thornfield Hall, he shows decision and acumen. *Jane Eyre*

DENT, MRS.: Colonel Dent's wife, is not showy but ladylike, with a pale, gentle face. Shows consideration for Jane Eyre, who is generally ignored by Rochester's other guests. *Jane Eyre*

DIGBY, DR.: Graham Bretton's Headmaster. *Villette*

DOAD O'BILLS: Finds liberty in the Methodist Chapel. *Shirley*

DOLORES: A dark, mutinous, Catalan pupil of Mme. Beck, disliked by her associates. She persists longest in disturbing the class until Lucy Snowe pushes her into a cupboard. *Villette*

DONNE, JOSEPH: Curate of Whinbury. Coldly phlegmatic, densely self-satisfied, he flaunts his Southern (Cockney) accent and despises his humbler parishioners, whose natural directness and tact contrast with his pseudo-culture. Courts Shirley Keeldar, who soon reprimands his complacency. After the novel ends, turns out an admirable though materialistic parson, through marrying a good wife. *Shirley*

DORLODOT, MME. LA BARONNE DE: Aunt of Colonel de Hamal. Her influence admits him to the school fête. *Villette*

DORLODOT, LA PETITE DE: A young pupil of Mlle. Reuter. She is escorted home when her maid does not arrive by Frances Henri, whose low status in the school is thus shown. *The Professor*

DRONSART, ADELE: A Belgian pupil of Mlle. Reuter. Stout, young, fresh and blooming, but Gorgon-like: 'vicious propensities in her eye; envy and panther-like deceit about her mouth.' Bad as many of her fellow pupils are, few are as bad as she. *The Professor*

E

EARNSHAW, MR.: Father of Hindley and Catherine, owner of Wuthering Heights, a kind man though rather severe.

Picks up the foundling Heathcliff from a Liverpool gutter and makes him a favourite in preference to his own son, against whom his mind is further poisoned by his pious servant Joseph. His strength leaves him suddenly and he becomes ailing and peevish. Does not understand jokes from his children so Catherine's high spirits also displease him. Dies quietly in his armchair. *Wuthering Heights*

EARNSHAW, MRS.: Wife of Mr. Earnshaw, resents his bringing Heathcliff into their home. Dies two years afterwards. *Wuthering Heights*

EARNSHAW, CATHERINE: Daughter of old Mr. Earnshaw of Wuthering Heights. As a child her spirits are always at high water mark; she is wilful, reckless and hardy. Inseparable from the foundling Heathcliff, both rough as savages, her contact with the refined, rich Lintons affects her tastes so that for a while she vaccillates between civilised behaviour with them and wild pursuits with Heathcliff. However when Heathcliff overhears her confession that he is now too degraded for her to marry and he leaves the district; she is left to recover alone from grief, illness, and weaker in nerves and body marries the gentle Edgar Linton. Their peaceful happiness is interrupted by the return of Heathcliff, now prosperous and educated, but still violent and passionately attached to Catherine. Her rage at her husband's jealousy brings on a brainfever but her partial recovery does not survive a passionate meeting with Heathcliff, and she dies giving birth to a daughter, Cathy. True to her threat never to rest till he joins her, she haunts Heathcliff's mind's eye up to his death, and afterwards country people say both their ghosts walk. In spite of their varying fortunes her love for Heathcliff remains constant, although much of the character otherwise alters, and like Heathcliff she is dangerously single-minded, though she lives in the present moment. *Wuthering Heights*

EARNSHAW, FRANCES: Hindley's wife, whom he brings home unexpectedly after his father's death following a secret marriage that suggests she is of no birth or fortune. Rather thin, but young, fresh-complexioned and bright-eyed, she is already consumptive and dies soon after giving birth to Hareton, after which Hindley becomes desperate with grief. *Wuthering Heights*

EARNSHAW, HARETON: Son of Hindley and Frances, nursed by Ellen Dean at first when his mother dies, later ignored by his father who is usually desperate and drunk. Grows up untaught and barbaric in spite of innate good qualities. When Hindley loses all the family lands and money to Heathcliff and dies, Hareton attaches himself to Heathcliff who is purposely impoverishing and degrading him as revenge for his own early ill-treatment by Hindley. The contempt of his cousin Catherine Linton humiliates him and inspires an attempt at self-education, checked by her further scorn. However when she is later confined to Wuthering Heights as the penniless widow of Heathcliff's son, he forgives her, learns to read, becomes civilised and when Heathcliff dies they marry. *Wuthering Heights*

EARNSHAW, HARETON: An ancestor of the Earnshaws, possibly the founder of Wuthering Heights, where his name and the date 1550 are carved. *Wuthering Heights*

EARNSHAW, HEATHCLIFF: A dead son of the Earnshaws, after whom the foundling Heathcliff is named. *Wuthering Heights*

EARNSHAW, HINDLEY: Brother of Catherine, son of old Mr. Earnshaw who favours the foundling Heathcliff at his expense. Goes to college and returns after his father's death with a wife, Frances, and at once degrades Heathcliff to a farm hand, separating him from Catherine. When Frances dies of consumption soon after giving birth to a son, Hareton, he turns desperate and gives himself up to dissipation. Takes pains to marry Catherine to the rich Edgar Linton. When Heathcliff returns, prosperous, educated and secretly bent on revenge, Hindley puts himself in his power by gambling away money and land to him, and is soon driven almost to madness. After attempting to kill his tormentor he drinks himself to death, possibly speeded by Heathcliff. *Wuthering Heights*

ELIZA: The Rev. Helstone's cook, competent and proud of her skill. *Shirley*

EMANUEL, JOSEF: Paul Emanuel's brother, a noted pianist but less forceful character. *Villette*

EMANUEL, M. PAUL CARL DAVID: Cousin of Mme. Beck, in whose boarding school he acts as visiting teacher of literature, though more permanently employed by Villette's 'Academy'. Although he replaces Dr. John as male lead in the second half of the novel, he appears little in the first part. However, his recommendation that Lucy Snowe be employed when she arrives destitute at the school is crucial to her fortunes. At first his irascible, undignified public behaviour amuses Lucy; later she learns to love his warmth and generosity. In his youth he is rejected by the rich family of the girl he loves, Justine-Marie, who enters a convent and soon afterwards dies. For her sake, when her family becomes poor, he supports them with half his income. His sentimental and financial involvement is revealed by Mme. Beck to discourage Lucy—unsuccessfully, as his attractions are confirmed by this new romantic dimension. He agrees to spend three years in Guadeloupe attending to family affairs as the price of his independence, but on his return voyage a storm threatens his ship—his survival is left uncertain.

Though his fiery, unreserved nature contrasts with Lucy's, both are destined to suffer and struggle stoically against adverse fate. *Villette*

ESHTON, MR.: A magistrate of The Leas near Thornfield Hall. He and his family accompany their guest Rochester back to Thornfield to form part of a house party. His white hair, dark eyebrows and whiskers give him the air of a *'père noble de théâtre'*. *Jane Eyre*

ESHTON, MRS.: Wife of Mr. Eshton, has evidently been a handsome woman and is well preserved still. Good-natured, has three daughters, two of whom go with her to Thornfield Hall. *Jane Eyre*

ESHTON, AMY: Eldest daughter of the Eshtons, fair, rather small, naïve and childlike, lively in manner. *Jane Eyre*

ESHTON, LOUISA: Second daughter of the Eshtons, fair, taller and more elegant than her sister, with a very pretty face. *Jane Eyre*

EULALIE: Pupil at Mlle. Reuter's school, sits in the front row. Tall, finely shaped, fair and stolid, she has acquired some mechanical knowledge in six years' schooling but still makes slovenly, silly mistakes. *The Professor*

EYRE, JANE: Orphaned as a baby by the death of her mother and clergyman father in an epidemic, Jane is taken in by her uncle Reed, and brought up after his death by his widow. Ill-treated by her cousins, despised by the servants, she is a reserved, introspective child, but upon her passionate retaliation to bullying is punished immediately by imprisonment in the haunted Red Room and subsequently by relegation to a semi-charitable boarding school, Lowood. Economy practised at the expense of the under-nourished pupils predisposes them to a typhus epidemic, in which many die. Jane, learning to tame her passions from her friend, the mild, consumptive Helen Burns, survives to become a teacher. At eighteen, when her mentor, the austere, intellectual Miss Temple, leaves to marry, she advertises for a post as private governess and is employed to teach Adèle Varens, the ward of Mr. Rochester. She is happy at Thornfield in spite of a mysterious presence on the third floor. After paying marked attentions to the beautiful proud Blanche Ingram, on purpose to confirm Jane's attraction through jealousy, Rochester proposes marriage. The wedding is dramatically interrupted by the news that Thornfield's third storey contains his living but insane wife. Refusing to become his mistress, Jane escapes by night, and losing her scanty luggage, is left destitute on the moors. Near starvation she is taken in by Diana, Mary and St. John Rivers, who nurse her then find her work as a village schoolmistress. The Rivers turn out to be Jane's cousins, whose rich uncle, John Eyre, has left all his fortune to her, which she at once redistributes among the four of them. Still pining for Rochester, she wavers when St. John insists she marry him (because she would be a more suitable helpmeet in his missionary vocation than the spoilt heiress he really loves) but hearing an uncanny telepathic summons from Rochester, she travels back to find Thornfield burnt down by the mad wife, now dead, and Rochester living as a recluse at Ferndean, maimed and blinded. They marry, he later partially recovers his sight and they have a son, Edward. Small, 'obscure, plain and little', Jane's attractions are mainly spiritual and intellectual (unlike the bulky materialistic female opponents—Mrs. Reed, Blanche, the madwoman—who cross her path) and the stoical sense of duty acquired at Lowood is always at odds with her originally passionate nature. *Jane Eyre*

EYRE, JOHN: Jane Eyre's uncle, a wine merchant in the West Indies and *deus ex machina* in the plot. Calls to enquire about Jane at Gateshead while she is away at school, and is later falsely told by Mrs. Reed that Jane has died of typhus, an impression she writes to correct while informing him of her prospective marriage to Rochester. He learns of the existence of Rochester's insane but living wife, whose family also live in the West Indies, and sends messages to prevent the bigamy. Dying of 'decline' soon afterwards, leaves his whole fortune to Jane and nothing to his other nieces and nephew, the Rivers. *Jane Eyre*

F

F——, LORD: One of the noblemen who attends Rosalie Murray's coming-out ball. Said to hate his wife, and is much struck by Rosalie, dances with her twice and is so complimentary that she has to snub him. Also his wife, very cross, especially at his attentions to Rosalie. *Agnes Grey*

F——, LADY: A married woman with whom Arthur Huntingdon has an intrigue before his marriage. *The Tenant of Wildfell Hall*

FAIRFAX, MRS. ALICE: Widow of the former vicar of Hay, a relative of Mr. Rochester, for whom she now keeps house at Thornfield Hall. She answers Jane Eyre's advertisement and employs her as governess to Rochester's ward Adèle Varens. Kindly though trite, she supplies motherly companionship if not mental stimulus for Jane. Does not know that the madwoman secretly confined in Thornfield is Rochester's wife, though she is uneasy about his attachment to Jane. After his attempted bigamy, Rochester becomes a recluse and pensions her off. *Jane Eyre*

FANNY: Servant at Briarfield Rectory. Kind to Caroline. *Shirley*

FANSHAWE, CAPTAIN: Ginevra's father, an officer on half-pay. Appears gentlemanly though languid. *Villette*

FANSHAWE, GINEVRA: Pupil of Mme. Beck, meets Lucy on the Channel Ferry and becomes friendly with her.

Dr. John is infatuated with her but she prefers the dandy Colonel de Hamal. Pretty, poor and vain, she coaxes gowns and jewellery from her rich chaperon and from Dr. John, but it is her sneers at his mother that complete his disillusionment. Elopes with de Hamal. Honesty is the redeeming virtue in her general selfishness which usually protects her from suffering: she goes on 'fighting the battle of life by proxy and on the whole suffering as little as any human being I have ever known'. *Villette*

FITZJAMES, CAPTAIN: A captain in the navy, a gallant officer and a good man. Marries Diana Rivers. *Jane Eyre*

FARREN, GRACE: William's wife, a 'raight cant body' and scrupulous housewife. Also, BEN, one of their children. *Shirley*

FARREN, WILLIAM: Hard-favoured but modest member of Barraclough's deputation. Moore shows typical harshness in repelling his sincere exposition of the workers' sufferings, but later obtains him gardening work with Mr. Yorke. Farren becomes friendly with Caroline. A quieter version of the independent Yorkshireman. *Shirley*

FRANK: Miss Marchmont's fiancé, dies shortly before their marriage. *Villette*

FREDERIC, MME.: A Frenchwoman who takes in Adèle Varens for a short time after her mother Céline abandons her, before Rochester takes Adèle to England. *Jane Eyre*

G

G——, JULIA and GEORGIANA: daughters of an English baronet, attend the school of Frances Crimsworth (née Henri) in Brussels. The *Professor*

G——, LORD: One of the noblemen who attends Rosalie Murray's coming-out ball and, being married already, does not merit her attentions. *Agnes Grey*

GALE, JOHN: A small clothier and former churchwarden, fortunately indulgent to the clergy as he is Mr. Donne's landlord. *Shirley*

GALE, MRS.: Donne's landlady, whose Yorkshire soul is revolted by the curates' presumption and incivility. Also, **ABRAHAM**, her six-year-old son who weeps when the curates leave him no remnant of spice cake. *Shirley*

GARRETT, MARY: A scholar at Jane Eyre's school at Morton who is absent during her mother's illness. *Jane Eyre*

GERARD, CONSTANTINE: Robert Moore's maternal grandfather. Member of an old business house he is ruined by unrest in Europe, especially the French Revolution. *Shirley*

GERARD, HORTENSE: Mother of Robert, Louis and Hortense Moore. Unites English and Flemish business houses by marrying Moore, Snr. Kept 'a hot kitchen of it in Antwerp'. *Shirley*

GIACINTA: An Italian girl who is successor to Céline Varens as Rochester's second mistress, singularly handsome but unprincipled and violent. He tires of her in three months, hating likewise the degradation of hiring a mistress (which Jane Eyre takes as a warning). *Jane Eyre*

GIBSON, MR.: Mrs. Reed's brother, who comes after her death to settle her affairs, order her funeral and invite her younger daughter Georgiana to live with him in London. *Jane Eyre*

GIBSON: MRS.: Wife of Mr. Gibson, who takes Eliza and Georgiana into society when they stay with her. *Jane Eyre*

GILL, MRS.: Shirley's housekeeper. At first cheats on the housekeeping bills, and is frequently forgiven: becomes devoted to Shirley. *Shirley*

GOTON: Flemish cook in Mme. Beck's school, with whom Lucy is a favourite. *Villette*

GRAHAM, MRS. HELEN: (*see* Huntingdon, Mrs. Helen)

GRAME, MR.: Sir Philip Nunnely's steward. *Shirley*

GRANBY, MR.: One of the best connected and most estimable residents in S——, grandson and heir to Sir Frederic Granby, soon consoles Rosamund Oliver for the loss of St. John Rivers' attentions, and marries her. *Jane Eyre*

GRANBY, SIR FREDERIC: Grandfather of Mr. Granby, gives up his house S—— Place to him when he marries. *Jane Eyre*

GRAVES, MR.: Dr. MacTurk's assistant. *Shirley*

GREAVES, MRS.: A decent servant of Arthur Huntingdon, who leaves after his wife departs and he deteriorates. *The Tenant of Wildfell Hall*

GREEN, MR.: Attends Rosalie Murray's coming-out ball, subsequently becomes her suitor but as he is of no family and a great stupid fellow, a mere country booby, though rich enough, he has no chance. After being refused continues to importune her in letters, and after her marriage is said to be heartbroken. *Agnes Grey*

GREEN, JANE and SUSAN: Sisters of Mr. Green, friends of Rosalie Murray, ignore Agnes Grey the governess. *Agnes Grey*

GREEN, JOHN: Clerk at Hay Church near Thornfield Hall, present at the interrupted wedding of Rochester and Jane Eyre. *Jane Eyre*

GREEN: Edgar Linton's lawyer who, bribed by Heathcliff, delays visiting the dying Edgar so that he cannot secure his daughter's income against fortune-hunters. *Wuthering Heights*

GREY, MRS.: Once governess to Blanche and Mary Ingram, too coarse and insensitive to be subjected to teasing by them. *Jane Eyre*

GREY, MISS: Maiden name of Mrs. Pryor (Mrs. Helstone), Shirley's companion-governess. *Shirley*

GREY, AGNES: Younger surviving daughter of the Rev. Richard Grey. The baby of the family, six years younger than her sister Mary, at eighteen she amazes them by wishing to become a governess to assist their fallen fortunes. Her first position with the Bloomfields is a failure, as she has not the authority to deal with her cold, hostile employers and their malicious, half-savage children, and she is dismissed within a year for lack of progress. Though mortified she goes next to the Murrays where, though unsuccessful with the two young boys, who are soon sent to school, she makes some impression on the coquettish Rosalie and the hoyden, Matilda. Lonely amid the uncongenial Murrays, she is delighted to meet the curate Mr. Weston, whose austere, unworldly benevolence she respects. Her hopes of his affection are disappointed by Rosalie's powerful attempts to attract him, but he seems unaffected. Agnes' father dies, partly from melancholia, and she goes to start a school with her widowed mother. When Mr. Weston becomes vicar of a nearby parish, they meet again and eventually marry. Not beautiful, with her marked features, ordinary dark brown hair, intellectual brow and expressive grey eyes, she is too diffident, honourable and gentle to educate her recalcitrant charges against their will, and fears at one point being numbed and brutalised by her superficial companions, appreciating the more evangelical earnestness of the reforming Mr. Weston. *Agnes Grey*

GREY, AUNT: Sister of Agnes' father Richard Grey, kind and prim, who recommends Agnes as governess to an acquaintance of her youth, Mrs. Bloomfield, whom she describes as a very nice person. (She is mistaken.) *Agnes Grey*

GREY, RICHARD: A clergyman of the North of England, marries Alice who is disinherited and disowned by her father. They have two daughters, Mary and Agnes. Neither tranquil nor cheerful by nature he blames himself for his wife's poverty but, on trying to restore her to fortune, loses all his money in a trading venture. This failure overwhelms him, and morbid self-reproach leads to obsession and illness. He dies some years later before Agnes, working away from home as a governess, can see him again. *Agnes Grey*

GREY, MRS. ALICE: Wife of the Rev. Richard Grey. The daughter of a rich squire, she leaves family and fortune to marry and is happy in her marriage and household duties. When her husband loses his money in his efforts to make up to her the wealth she has never really regretted, she proves capable of even the roughest household work. His morbid depression leads to illness and death, but she refuses to live with her married daughter Mary and sets up a school with Agnes, which she continues after Agnes' marriage. Her active, managing character shows up the perversity of her husband's self-reproaches: far from suffering, she is the kind of woman who is much happier when busy and efficient. *Agnes Grey*

GREY, MARY: Daughter of Richard and Alice Grey, older than her sister Agnes by about six years. A quiet, capable girl, well-educated by her mother, she is a talented painter, earning a little money in this way after the loss of her father's fortune. Later marries a clergyman, Mr. Richardson. *Agnes Grey*

GRIMSBY: The worst of Arthur Huntingdon's friends, a

confirmed and lucky gambler, a base, malignant, low-minded man, the most assiduous in trying to re-corrupt Lord Lowborough. After Huntingdon's death, he goes from bad to worse, and at last meets his end in a drunken brawl. *The Tenant of Wildfell Hall*

GRYCE, MISS: A heavy, Welsh teacher at Lowood school who shares Jane Eyre's room when she too becomes a teacher. Snores habitually. *Jane Eyre*

GUSTAVE: A boy attending a school next door to Mme. Beck's, nephew of Col. de Hamal who on the pretext of visiting him gains access to Mme. Beck's garden. *Villette*

H

HALFORD: The recipient of Gilbert Markham's history of the tenant of Wildfell Hall. After the novel closes he becomes Markham's close friend and husband of his sister Rose. *The Tenant of Wildfell Hall*

HALL, CYRIL: Vicar of Nunnely. Forty-five years old, a scholar, near-sighted, frank and simple. The most consistently religious of the clergy, he affords practical charity as well as spiritual advice. *Shirley*

HALL, MARGARET: Sister of the Rev. Cyril Hall, a kindly, bespectacled old maid. *Shirley*

HALL, PEARSON: Related to Cyril Hall, he is Shirley's family solicitor. *Shirley*

HAMAL, COLONEL; COUNT ALFRED DE: Rival to Dr. John Bretton for Ginevra's favours, eventually elopes with and marries her. To meet her within the school he disguises himself as the ghostly nun. A straight-nosed, very

correct featured little dandy, trim as a doll, he is as superficial and selfish as Ginevra herself.

Also, ALFRED FANSHAWE DE BASSOMPIERRE DE
HAMAL, their son. *Villette*

HANNAH: Family servant, once the nurse of the Rivers, a
loyal, brusque, typical Yorkshirewoman, who to protect
her mistresses, suspecting thieves, tries to turn away Jane
Eyre who collapses starving on their doorstep. Is later won
over by Jane's neatness and plain speaking. *Jane Eyre*

HARDMAN, MRS.: Mrs. Pryor's early employer, recommends
her to cultivate profound humility and self-effacement.
Shirley

HARDMAN, MISS: Daughter of Mrs. Hardman, considers
the ruin of certain gentlemen's families providential to
maintain the supply of poor but educated governesses for
the aristocracy. *Shirley*

HARGRAVE, MRS.: A hard, pretentious, worldly-minded
woman, mother of Walter, Millicent and Esther. Squanders
much of her modest income on lavish appearances, and is
miserly with the rest. Her aim is to make rich matches for
her daughters, regardless of their happiness, and she
spoils her son, encouraging his selfishness and expensive
habits. After her children marry, is expected to go and live
on her jointure. *The Tenant of Wildfell Hall*

HARGRAVE, ESTHER: Millicent's younger sister, light-
hearted and more spirited. Resists her mother's pressure to
marry a rich old man. Becomes Helen Huntingdon's
friend, and is almost embittered by her family's constant
persuasion to marry, though holding out through obstinacy,
when she meets and marries Helen's brother Frederick
Lawrence. *The Tenant of Wildfell Hall*

HARGRAVE, MILLICENT: Sister of Walter Hargrave,
cousin to Annabella Wilmot, she develops a strong

admiration for Helen Huntingdon. Is overpersuaded to marry wild, reckless Ralph Hattersley, and comes to love him in spite of his drunken excesses. A small, pretty woman with light brown ringlets, she sometimes irritates her husband by her submissiveness and is too long-suffering to point out her injuries. Helen's more vigorous representations persuade her to be less timid and him to be more considerate, so at last his reformation brings her happiness. Has a fine family of stalwart sons and blooming daughters. *The Tenant of Wildfell Hall*

HARGRAVE, WALTER: Friend of Arthur Huntingdon, brother of Millicent and Esther. While Arthur neglects his wife Helen, he tries to win her affection by sympathy, compliments and hints against her erring husband, and his restraint of Arthur's excesses has the same ulterior motive. Rejected by Helen once, he returns to the attack with such violence that she has to oppose him with a knife. Then leaves her house and later fails to marry a rich widow for control of her fortune. Succeeds in marrying a less rich, very plain forty-year-old spinster. An old servant remembers him as spoilt, proud and wilful from boyhood: his sisters' admiration overlooks his selfish extravagance at their expense. *The Tenant of Wildfell Hall*

HARRIET (HURST, MRS.): Nursemaid to the little Pauline Home, still her maid later in Europe. *Villette*

HARTLEY, MICHAEL: The Antinomian weaver, crazed and a drunkard. Shoots Robert Moore as an example to all tyrants. Is recognised but not pursued by the regenerate Moore, but dies of *delirium tremens* a year later. *Shirley*

HATFIELD, MR.: Rector of Horton. A fashionable, worldly cleric, who curls his hair and wears silk gowns, lavender gloves and sparkling rings when preaching, and neglects his humble parishioners for his wealthy neighbours; he ignores Agnes Grey because she is only a governess. He is led on by the beautiful Rosalie Murray to propose to her, so that she can mortify his vanity by refusing him, though thereafter his pride prevents him showing his feelings. Later he marries an elderly spinster, weighing her heavy purse against her faded charms. *Agnes Grey*

HATTERSLEY, HELEN: Daughter of Millicent and Ralph, a merry child who grows up to marry Helen Huntingdon's son Arthur. *The Tenant of Wildfell Hall*

HATTERSLEY, MILLICENT: *see* Hargrave, Millicent

HATTERSLEY, RALPH: Son of a rich banker, one of Arthur Huntingdon's cronies, indulges in drunken revelry, but Helen Huntingdon comes to find that 'this boorish ruffian, coarse and brutal as he was, shone like a glow-worm in the dark among its fellow worms'. He marries Helen's friend Millicent whom he loves though her sweet submissiveness tries his patience and increases his selfishness. Later tires of his friends and, being told by Helen how much his wife suffers from his behaviour, decides to reform. Later he travels to visit the repentant Huntingdon on his death-bed, and is impressed and confirmed in his reformation. Remains in his north country home indulging his natural taste for country pursuits, and has outstanding success with horse breeding, aided by his inheritance on his father's death. *The Tenant of Wildfell Hall*

HATTERSLEY, RALPH (THE YOUNGER): Eldest of Hattersley's stalwart sons. *The Tenant of Wildfell Hall*

HEATHCLIFF: Found by Mr. Earnshaw in the gutters of Liverpool, dirty and almost inarticulate, he is brought up at Wuthering Heights, where he usurps the affection due to Earnshaw's son Hindley, but is inseparable from his daughter, the wild, spirited Catherine. When Earnshaw dies and his enemy Hindley returns home, Heathcliff is degraded from companion to farmhand. Very dark, with black hair and threatening deep-set black eyes, he becomes rough and boorish, and when Catherine, by befriending the gentle Edgar Linton, learns to deplore his degradation, he runs away. He returns a dignified, self-possessed man of means, though as ruthless and violent as ever. Winning all Hindley's money as revenge for old injuries he visits Catherine, now married to Edgar, whose sister Isabella later elopes with him. Suspecting his motives towards both Isabella and Catherine, Edgar quarrels with him, thus making Catherine so ill that only with difficulty can Heathcliff manage to see her and their meeting causes another crisis culminating in her death in childbirth. His anguish is succeeded by plans for revenge. He marries her daughter Cathy to his son Linton, who dies soon afterwards. Heathcliff inherits the land and fortune of the Lintons, meanwhile degrading Hindley's son Hareton to a servant. However, his growing obsession with visions of the dead Catherine weaken his interest in vengeance, and finally giving himself up to the visions he wastes away and dies. Though his origins and his later acquisition of wealth and education remain mysterious, his embitterment and his diabolic cruelty are the results of perverse treatment: it is his violent single-mindedness that, like Catherine's, brings a trail of destruction on weaker beings. *Wuthering Heights*

HEATHCLIFF, LINTON: Son of Heathcliff and Isabella, born a few months after she runs away. At thirteen, when his mother dies, he goes to her brother's home but has to be given up the next day to Heathcliff, who plans to revenge himself on his old enemy Hindley Earnshaw by making his own son master of Hindley's son and lands. He is bitterly disappointed when Linton grows up a peevish, sickly, timid boy. Lack of sympathy makes him selfish and malicious, and he has to be terrorised into marrying his cousin Cathy, by which he (in effect, his father) gains her personal fortune, and retaliates by ill-treating her. He is allowed to die with only Cathy to nurse him. Fair and blue-eyed, he resembles in appearance his uncle Edgar Linton, whose refinement and gentleness is weakened in him to fussiness and apathy. *Wuthering Heights*

HELSTONE, JAMES: Caroline's father, ill-treats her mother, neglects her, drinks. Dies when Caroline is eight. A man-tiger, he is 'handsome, dissolute, soft, treacherous, courteous, cruel'. *Shirley*

HELSTONE, CAROLINE: As much the heroine as the eponymous Shirley, Caroline is a shy pensive girl of eighteen, brought up by her uncle the Rector after her father's death ten years earlier (her mother's whereabouts unknown). In love with her penurious cousin Robert Moore, her lack of fortune deters him and his neglect drives her to a despairing refuge in a wholly religious life. Unlike Shirley, she has not the resilience to bear depression well, and a fever almost kills her. Her will to live depends on human warmth, hitherto lacking in the treatment of her generous but brusque uncle or in a life of good works. This warmth is newly supplied when Mrs. Pryor is revealed as her long lost mother. Caroline recovers, and Robert Moore decides to marry her even before peace brings prosperity. Caroline learns by suffering the necessity of facing harsh reality. *Shirley*

HELSTONE, THE REV. MATTHEWSON: Rector of Briar-field, Caroline's uncle, an upright falcon-like man, copper-faced. Sociable in company, he is taciturn at home, believing all women to be fools. Marries Mary Cave, who dies after five years of marriage. Provides well for Caroline, but has no patience with 'sympathy—sentiment—some of these indefinite abstractions'. As far right politically as the equally harsh Mr. Yorke is to the left. *Shirley*

HENRI, FRANCES EVANS: Daughter of an English mother and a Swiss father, brought up by her aunt in some poverty.

Has learned to mend lace, by which she earns money for furthering her education, and hopes to become a teacher. While teaching needlework in Mlle. Reuter's school, she attends William Crimsworth's classes in English. Her originality and her well-pronounced if faulty English attract his attention, and eventually they fall in love. Mlle. Reuter, jealous, takes advantage of Frances' aunt being ill to dismiss her, and conceals her address from Crimsworth, hoping to separate them, but Frances meets him by chance near her aunt's grave. Shortly afterwards she becomes a French teacher in an English school in Brussels, and marries Crimsworth when he too finds a new and remunerative position. They have a son, Victor, and she finally achieves her dream of living in England. Thin, pale and sensitive, she has all the frankness and integrity that Mlle. Reuter lacks, and equal intelligence and determination: she continues teaching even after the birth of her son, and successfully launches her own school. *The Professor*

HENRI, 'TANTE' JULIENNE: Frances Henri's aunt, brings her up but cannot afford to pay for advanced education from her small annuity. Is persuaded by Frances to leave Switzerland for Belgium, where she dies. Crimsworth finds Frances after their separation weeping beside her grave. *The Professor*

HIGGINS, GEORGE: A Horton villager who is likely to be frightened out of his sabbath evening walks by the vicar's gloomier sermons. *Agnes Grey*

HOBSON, MR.: The third tradesman with whom Agnes' father Richard Grey runs up a bill while hoping to make his fortune by trade. *Agnes Grey*

HOGG, MRS.: Malone's exasperated landlady. *Shirley*

HOLMES, BETTY: An old cottager whose thirty years'

indulgence in a pipe of tobacco is likely to be censored in the vicar's gloomier sermons. *Agnes Grey*

HOME DE BASSOMPIERRE, MR.: Part Scottish, part French, he is a big, shrewd, blunt man, of scientific interests. He leaves his daughter Paulina with his distant relative, Mrs. Bretton, while travelling for his health. Later inherits a fortune and French title, is a doting father, reluctant to let his daughter grow up. *Villette*

HOME DE BASSOMPIERRE, PAULINA: Stays with Mrs. Bretton, her distant relative, as a child of eight while her father travels, and is saved from pining by developing an attachment to the sixteen-year-old John Graham Bretton, which he returns only casually. The tables are turned later when he courts her in Villette after her father has inherited wealth and a title. Their meeting is dramatic, as he rescues her from a theatre fire; her initial coolness is overcome, as is the possessiveness of her father, and they eventually marry. From a quaint, self-contained child she becomes a modest, thoughtful, well-controlled (and beautiful) young woman. Her reserve and delicacy contrast with her cousin Ginevra Fanshawe's bouncing superficiality, as her good fortune contrasts with Lucy's struggles: 'Some lives are thus blessed—it is God's will.' *Villette*

HOME, MRS. GINEVRA: Late wife of Mr. Home. A pretty giddy woman, neglects her child and husband, is separated from him by consent, dies of a cold caught at a ball. Ginevra Fanshawe, her niece, is said to resemble her. *Villette*

HORSEFALL, ZILLAH, MRS.: The nurse attending Robert Moore after the shooting. No woman but a dragon, a giantess and a dram-drinker. Nevertheless, drunk or sober, she obeys Dr. MacTurk implicitly. *Shirley*

HORTENSE: Pupil at Mlle. Reuter's school, sits in the front

row. Stout and ungraceful, she is vivacious but not sensible. *The Professor*

HOUSEKEEPER: A woman formerly of Gimmerton, known to Ellen Dean, who keeps house at Wuthering Heights from Hindley's death until two years after Linton Heathcliff goes there. *Wuthering Heights*

HUNSDEN, HUNSDEN YORKE: A mill-owner of an old family, heir to Hunsden Wood. An original character, he tries to goad William Crimsworth into leaving the oppressive employment of his brother Edward, against whom he inflames public opinion, thus causing a quarrel and rupture between the two brothers. Affects William's destiny further by suggesting he should teach in Belgium, writing him a letter of recommendation. Visits William occasionally in Brussels, salting all his benefits with sarcasm. Later inherits the family mansion where he retires, and close to which William and his wife make their eventual home. Sardonic and cynical, he affects bluntness, and though sensitive himself he ignores others' sensibility. He and Crimsworth are drawn together by a common sense of wrong but (as also in the case of Charles) Crimsworth feels a superior capacity for generous feeling. *The Professor*

HUNTINGDON, ARTHUR (THE YOUNGER): Son of Arthur and Helen Huntingdon. In infancy is encouraged to drink and swear by his father who also instals his mistress as the governess; mainly for his sake his mother takes him away secretly on her flight. Grows into a fine young man and marries Helen Hattersley. *The Tenant of Wildfell Hall*

HUNTINGDON, ARTHUR: Handsome, charming young man with blue eyes and golden curls (under which his skull sinks rather alarmingly), marries the beautiful Helen Lawrence, progressively revealing himself as a selfish profligate. First neglects Helen then enters on a two-year love affair with Lady Lowborough, and rapidly becomes addicted to drink. When he encourages his little son to join his drinking parties and brings home his new mistress as governess, his wife leaves him, taking the child. About a year later he is so weakened by intemperance that a hunting accident entails serious illness, his injuries become gangrenous and he dies in a state of horror. Indulgence in drink is only one aspect of his general self-indulgence and callousness to those about him. *The Tenant of Wildfell Hall*

HUNTINGDON, HELEN: Née Lawrence, also known as Mrs. Graham. A wilful, beautiful girl with black hair and grey eyes, talented as a painter, she marries the charming, irresponsible Arthur Huntingdon, hoping to reform his frivolity: instead she finds he is selfish and profligate. She struggles against his tendency to drink, giving up in disgust when he deceives her with Lady Lowborough. Her strong character becomes harder when he attempts to corrupt their little son Arthur too with wine at adult drinking bouts, and instals his mistress as governess. Deciding therefore to leave him, Helen secretly escapes to Wildfell Hall, owned by her brother Frederick Lawrence, where she lives secluded under the name Mrs. Graham. Inquisitive neighbours visit her, including Gilbert Markham who falls in love with her, believing her a widow. Secret visits from her brother cause a scandal and to dispel Gilbert's jealousy she reveals her history to him. Summoned to Huntingdon's death-bed she nurses him and tries to turn his horror of death into repentance. After his death she inherits a rich property from her uncle and goes to live there with her son and aunt, but when Gilbert visits her she removes his scruples about her wealth and they marry. Though her strength of character leads her into difficulties by defying reason and good advice it also enables her to endure and resist the evils of her situation, and her religious feeling preserves her from permanent embitterment. *The Tenant of Wildfell Hall*

HURST, MRS.: *see* Harriet

I

INGRAM, THE DOWAGER BARONESS: Mother of Lord Ingram, Blanche and Mary. Very tall, between forty and fifty, a splendid woman of her age except for an expression of almost insupportable haughtiness, her features not only inflated and darkened but even furrowed by pride. Blanche already resembles her. *Jane Eyre*

INGRAM, BLANCHE: Elder daughter of Baroness Ingram. Very tall, well built and beautiful with black hair and dark eyes and skin—in all points the opposite of Jane Eyre. Rochester's houseparty is a pretext for his flirtation with her, to rouse Jane's jealousy as a way to confirm her love for him. Very proud, spirited and selfish, she is also mercenary: once convinced his fortune is smaller than she supposed, she will have no more to do with him, being materialistic in both charms and outlook. *Jane Eyre*

INGRAM, MARY: Younger daughter of Baroness Ingram, as tall as her sister Blanche but slimmer, milder in appearance and less spirited. Statuesque in more ways than one, she languidly accepts the attentions of one of the Messrs. Lynn. *Jane Eyre*

INGRAM, THEODORE, LORD: Son of the dowager Lady Ingram, very tall and handsome but apathetic—'more length of limb than vivacity of blood or vigour of brain'. At Rochester's houseparty he flirts with Amy Eshton. *Jane Eyre*

ISABELLE: A pupil of Mme. Beck, an 'odd blunt little creature' who voices the general Catholic opinion that Lucy should be burnt as a heretic to avoid burning in hell. *Villette*

ISIDORE: Ginevra Fanshawe's name for Dr. John Bretton when he is her suitor. *Villette*

J

JACKSON, MR.: A tradesman with whom Agnes' father Richard Grey runs up a bill while expecting to make a large fortune by trade. *Agnes Grey*

JACKSON, THOMAS: An eccentric old villager at Horton, usually at odds with Nancy Browne, a breach healed when, on Mr. Weston's advice, she cultivates benevolence by knitting him stockings. He is likely to have his conscience and hope of resurrection shaken by the vicar's gratuitously menacing sermons. *Agnes Grey*

JACOB: A passer-by or labourer, near at hand when Eliza Milward tells Gilbert Markham that Helen Huntingdon is to be married. *The Tenant of Wildfell Hall*

JEM: *see* Wood, Mark (though he may be another member of the Wood family)

JENNY: Old Mr. Linton's servant. *Wuthering Heights*

JOHN, DR.: *see* Bretton, John Graham

JOHN: Mr. Rochester's coachman, a taciturn man and a slow driver, who with his wife Mary the cook, goes to Ferndean Manor to look after the blinded and maimed Rochester when Thornfield Hall has been burnt down. *Jane Eyre*

JOHN: Shirley's servant. *Shirley*

JOHN: Arthur Huntingdon's servant. *The Tenant of Wildfell Hall*

JOHN: Old Mr. Linton's servant at Thrushcross Grange. *Wuthering Heights*

JOHN OF MALLY'S OF HANNAH'S OF DEB'S: Supposed sweetheart of Sarah, the Moore's servant. *Shirley*

JOHNSTONE, AGNES and **CATHERINE:** Pupils at Lowood school, attract Mr. Brocklehurst's censure by having a second clean tucker in a week (against the rules) when invited out to tea. *Jane Eyre*

JONES, MR.: A dried-up bookseller in Paternoster Row, who seems to Lucy the greatest of beings. *Villette*

JOSEPH: Old servant at Wuthering Heights, 'the wearisomest, self-righteous Pharisee that ever ransacked a Bible to rake the promises to himself and fling the curses to his neighbours'. Gains influence over old Mr. Earnshaw by his piety, and makes trouble between him and his children. He and Nelly are the only servants to stay after Hindley Earnshaw loses his wife and turns to dissipation. When Heathcliff takes up residence there too he varies between pious horror and shocked resignation until the death of Hindley, whose son Hareton he then flatters and spoils, regarding his faults as Heathcliff's responsibility. When young Catherine marries Heathcliff's son, he is credulous of her pretences of witchcraft and horrified when, widowed, she is to marry his favourite, Hareton. Rejoices maliciously before praying at Heathcliff's death. *Wuthering Heights*

JOSEPH: A groom or coachman at Horton Lodge, whose company Matilda Murray prefers to her governess's. *Agnes Grey*

JOUBERT, MME.: Once governess to Blanche and Mary Ingram, subjected by them to teasing and disobedience, the more because she is easily infuriated. *Jane Eyre*

JULIENNE, 'TANTE': *see* Henri, Julienne

JUSTINE-MARIE: Once betrothed to Paul Emanuel she is separated from him by her rich family. Loyal, though not rebellious, she refuses other suitors, becomes a nun, and soon afterwards dies. Her memory is exploited by her family and friends to keep Mr. Paul unattached. Mme. Beck and Lucy both consider her character insipid. *Villette*

K

KEELDAR, CHARLES CAVE: Shirley's father, dies some time before her majority. *Shirley*

KEELDAR, SHIRLEY: Appears half-way through the novel and shares the honours as heroine with Caroline. An heiress, young and beautiful, she is even more enviable for her health and resilience. She owns the mill Robert Moore rents and soon attracts him, but when he proposes marriage for mercenary motives she indignantly reprimands him, for she is already in love with his brother, Louis, tutor to her cousin Henry Sympson. He is more modest and scrupulous than Robert but is eventually pressed to declare himself. Already mature and realistic, Shirley only has to suffer the mild anxiety as to Louis's intentions and an intense but short suspense about the bite of a rabid dog, bravely self-cauterised, and she bears loneliness better than Caroline because of her innate zest for life. Defying the worldly protests of the Sympsons, she marries Louis. *Shirley*

KENNETH, DR.: A plain, rough man, attends the inhabitants

of Wuthering Heights and Thrushcross Grange. Succeeds in bringing the elder Catherine Linton round from her brain fever. At one time the drinking companion of Hindley Earnshaw, who soon becomes too wild for him. *Wuthering Heights*

KING, MRS.: William Crimsworth's landlady in the town of X——; regards him highly for his steadiness and quietness. *The Professor*

KINT, MME.: Mme. Beck's mother. *Villette*

KINT, VICTOR: Mme. Beck's brother. *Villette*

KINT and VANDAM: Two honest but stupid Flemish ushers who have to supervise the pupils in leisure time as well as at lessons. M. Pelet's contempt and callousness towards them as beasts of burden shocks William Crimsworth and casts a suspicious light on his suave character. *The Professor*

KOSLOW, AURELIA: A German-Russian pupil at Mlle. Reuter's school, large, well-corseted and grubby, she is deplorably ignorant and ill-informed after twelve years at school. Aims her coquetry at Crimsworth in gestures, glances and grunts. *The Professor*

L

LABASSECOUR, KING OF: A man of fifty, a little bowed, a little grey, his face showing obsessive melancholia. *Villette*

LABASSECOUR, QUEEN OF: A mild, thoughtful, graceful woman, rather young. Also DINDONNEAU, DUC DE: prince of Labassecour, her eldest son. *Villette*

LA MALLE, MLLE.: A pupil at Mme. Beck's school, whose piano lesson is one of many to interrupt M. Paul's class. *Villette*

LANGWEILIG, MR.: A German Moravian minister who bores Mr. Sykes to sleep at a Bible Society meeting. *Shirley*

LAWRENCE, FREDERICK: Squire of Lindenhope, whose family lives in Wildfell Hall until they build a more convenient mansion. Dark-haired with shy hazel eyes, he is friendly with Gilbert Markham, but is too cold, reserved and self-contained for intimacy. Lets the Hall to a mysterious widow who in fact is his sister Helen escaping from her drunken husband. His visits arouse jealousy in Gilbert Markham who strikes and injures him. Though reconciled when the truth is known, he does not help Gilbert's suit even after her husband's death. While staying with his sister he meets and marries Esther Hargrave. His failure to assist Gilbert and Helen is due not to hostility but to his peculiar reticence and passivity, and a morbid delicacy that makes him an unsatisfactory friend. *The Tenant of Wildfell Hall*

LEAH: Housemaid at Thornfield Hall, a nice girl though no companion to the housekeeper Mrs. Fairfax: knows of the confinement of the madwoman on the third floor, though not her identity. *Jane Eyre*

LEAVEN, ROBERT: Mrs. Reed's coachman at Gateshead, kind, for he lets the child Jane Eyre ride her cousin's pony. Marries Bessie Lee, the nursemaid; brings Jane to Mrs. Reed's death-bed. Also, BOBBIE, JANE, and a baby, their children. *Jane Eyre*

LEAVEN, BESSIE: *see* Lee, Bessie

LEDRU, M.: Music master at Mlle. Reuter's school whom, though a married man of near fifty, she does not trust among her pupils. *The Professor*

LEE, BESSIE: Nursery maid to the Reed family at Gateshead Hall, smart, capable and good-natured but quick-tempered and impatient. Takes a liking to the child Jane Eyre, who prefers her to everyone else in the house, probably because she is the only one with the capacity for spontaneous kindly feeling. Sees her off to Lowood school, where she visits her eight years later. Summons Jane from Thornfield to Mrs. Reed's death-bed. Marries the Reed's coachman Robert Leaven and has three children. *Jane Eyre*

LEIGH, MRS.: Once a good-natured, comely but dull schoolfellow of Lucy Snowe, transformed by wifehood and motherhood into real beauty and kindness. She forgets Lucy, who is equally changed by her different fate. Also, CHARLES, her little boy, educated by a French nursemaid. *Villette*

LEIGHTON, MR.: Clergyman at the church attended by Helen Huntingdon's aunt and uncle. *The Tenant of Wildfell Hall*

LINTON, MR.: Owner of Thrushcross Grange, father of Edgar and Isabella. Catherine Earnshaw is caught straying in his gardens. Lectures her brother on taking better care of her. Dies of a fever caught from Catherine. *Wuthering Heights*

LINTON, MRS. MARY: Mother of Edgar and Isabella, deplores their possible contamination by Heathcliff. Visits Catherine Earnshaw when ill of a fever, and takes her home with her to recover, but this kindness leads to her catching the fever, of which she and her husband die within a few days of each other. *Wuthering Heights*

LINTON, CATHERINE, MRS.: Née Earnshaw, *see* Earnshaw, Catherine

LINTON, CATHERINE: Daughter of Edgar and Catherine Linton, her mother dies giving birth to her. A sickly child at seven months, she grows up a beauty, with her mother's dark eyes and her father's fair curls. She is high-spirited, though not rough, wilful, intensely affectionate, but also mild and pensive. An accidental visit to Wuthering Heights, where her cousin Linton lives, involves her in his father Heathcliff's plans to marry them in order to gain her private fortune and spite her father, his enemy. Held prisoner at the Heights she is compelled to marry Linton hastily to return to her father who is dying. Afterwards, penniless and under Heathcliff's domination, she is widowed and leads a friendless life until she wins over her other cousin Hareton, an illiterate boor, teaches and civilises him. After Heathcliff's death they marry. *Wuthering Heights*

LINTON, EDGAR: Son of old Mr. Linton, owner of Thrush-cross Grange, a fair, blue-eyed gentle boy who becomes infatuated with the spirited Catherine Earnshaw, out-shines the rough, overworked Heathcliff by his appearance, wealth and amiability, and marries her after Heathcliff's disappearance and her weakening illness confirm her attraction to him. After six months' peaceful happiness his jealousy is roused by Heathcliff's return and one quarrel leads to his wife's brainfever. He nurses her devotedly, only to see her precarious convalescence interrupted by a passionate visit from Heathcliff, followed at once by her death in childbirth. His grief is solaced by care for his daughter Cathy, whose later love for his nephew and heir Linton Heathcliff he at first opposes through hatred of Heathcliff. Later a cold settles on his lungs and he dies hoping that she will be provided for by that marriage after all. Gentle and benevolent, his sweetness to his wife is partly the yielding of a weaker, timid nature. *Wuthering Heights*

LINTON, ISABELLA: Sister of Edgar. As a charming young lady of eighteen, infantile in manners, fair-haired and blue-eyed, she falls in love with Heathcliff, who elopes with her to spite her brother, then ill-treats her. Her attachment is due to romantic ignorance rather than real spirit, though her subsequent stay at Wuthering Heights has its usual effect of embittering and hardening her. After a particularly ferocious fight between Heathcliff and his host, Hindley Earnshaw, she runs away and settles near London where after a few months her son Linton is born. She dies thirteen years later. *Wuthering Heights*

LLOYD, MR.: An apothecary, summoned by Mrs. Reed to treat her orphan niece Jane Eyre, who faints with terror when locked for punishment in a supposedly haunted room. This shows Jane's status, as he is usually called in to the servants, while a qualified physician treats the Reeds themselves. A hard-featured but good-natured man, he recommends that Jane be sent away to school, ostensibly for a change of air but probably because he has a shrewd idea of her ill-treatment by the Reeds. Somehow he is known to the headmistress of her school and is later called upon to vindicate her character against the slanders that follow her there. *Jane Eyre*

LOCKWOOD, MR.: Tenant of Thrushcross Grange, to whom his housekeeper Ellen Dean tells the story of Wuthering Heights. Withdrawing perversely from a love affair he seeks solitude but is intrigued by his misanthropic landlord Heathcliff and his beautiful widowed daughter-in-law Catherine, the more when, spending a night with them, he is terrified by dreams of her mother's ghost. Tempted to acquaintance by her beauty and sad history, he is deterred from staying by the wildness of northern winter and only returns nine months later to find her about to marry her cousin Hareton Earnshaw. Attracted by the prospect of solitude and wild simplicity, he is appalled when confronted with the real isolation and savage wilderness of Wuthering Heights and its inhabitants. *Wuthering Heights*

LOWBOROUGH, LORD: One of Arthur Huntingdon's friends, a desperate man who dissipates his fortune by gambling and other excesses, thereby losing his fiancée, keeps trying to stop gambling and drinking against the temptations of his friends, and, given to melancholy, gets caught in a round of indulgence and repentance. Courts the heiress Annabella Wilmot, first for her money, but afterwards falling in love with her. Disappointed by her scorn when he reforms, he becomes suicidal when he discovers she is Huntingdon's mistress. When she elopes with another lover he divorces her, and marries a woman of his own age whose good sense, benevolence and cheerfulness bring him happiness. Has two children, a son and little Annabella. *The Tenant of Wildfell Hall*

LOWBOROUGH, LADY: *see* Wilmot, Annabella

LOWBOROUGH, LADY (THE SECOND): A woman of between thirty and forty, remarkable for genuine good sense, active piety, and a fund of cheerful spirits. Becomes an invaluable wife to Lord Lowborough and an excellent mother to his children. *The Tenant of Wildfell Hall*

LOWBOROUGH, ANNABELLA (LITTLE): Daughter of the first Lady Lowborough, but only nominally of her husband, who is torn between fondness for the child herself and disgust at her paternity. *The Tenant of Wildfell Hall*

LUCIA: A dark, beautiful, triumphant and independent woman, whose portrait in miniature is carved by Hunsden and whom he compares with Frances Crimsworth's fine, pale, unobtrusive beauty. *The Professor*

LUCIEN, M.: Character in the school play acted by Lucy. *Villette*

LUPTON, MRS.: Guest at Edward Crimsworth's birthday dance. A stout person with a turban, he regards with ill-founded complacency Hunsden's attentions to her daughter, Sarah Martha. *The Professor*

LUPTON, SARAH MARTHA: A guest at Edward Crimsworth's birthday dance. A tall, well-made, full-formed, dashingly dressed young woman, whom Yorke Hunsden flatters by his attentions during the evening, without serious intention. *The Professor*

LYNN, SIR GEORGE: A very big, very fresh-looking country gentleman, elected member of parliament for Millcote. One of the party accompanying Mr. Rochester from Mr. Eshton's house to Thornfield Hall. *Jane Eyre*

LYNN, LADY: Wife of Sir George, a large stout personage, very erect, very haughty-looking. Spends her time with Lady Ingram. *Jane Eyre*

LYNN, FREDERICK and HENRY: Sons of Sir George, very dashing sparks indeed, devote themselves to Mary Ingram and Louisa Eshton. *Jane Eyre*

M

MACTURK, DR. (SNR.): Local doctor, abrupt at best, at worst, savage, attends Moore. Is skilful and 'less of a humbug than Dr. Rile'. Also MACTURK, DR. (JNR.): his son, an interesting facsimile of himself. *Shirley*

MALONE, PETER AUGUSTUS: Curate of Briarfield. Irish, besottedly arrogant, quarrelsome and clumsy, he courts first Caroline then Shirley. He ends in some disgrace that the author refuses to reveal. *Shirley*

MANN, MISS: An old maid of gorgon-like gaze and censorious habit, but closer acquaintance reveals she is ugly and embittered through appalling sufferings and ill through unselfish nursing. An example for good and evil to Caroline Helstone. *Shirley*

MANON and LOUISON: Flemish-speaking maids of Paulina Home de Bassompierre. *Villette*

MARCHMONT, MR.: Cousin and heir to the Miss Marchmont who once employed Lucy. Conscience-stricken after a grave illness, he sends money to Lucy, probably following some informal instructions left by his cousin, hitherto suppressed. *Villette*

MARCHMONT, MISS MARIA: A woman of fortune but a rheumatic cripple. Grave through suffering, irritable and exacting, but stoical in pain, she becomes Lucy Snowe's friend. She has lost her fiancé in a riding accident thirty years previously, and has been crippled for twenty years. *Villette*

MARKHAM, MR.: Gilbert Markham's father, a sort of gentleman farmer who thinks ambition the surest road to ruin and change but another word for destruction. Exhorts Gilbert with his dying breath to follow in his footsteps. *The Tenant of Wildfell Hall*

MARKHAM, MRS.: Gilbert Markham's mother, a notable housewife, proud of her ale, butter and cheese, who spoils her sons. Reproves Gilbert's flirtation with Eliza Millward and takes much persuasion to approve his marriage to Helen Huntingdon. *The Tenant of Wildfell Hall*

MARKHAM, FERGUS: Younger brother of Gilbert, an unmannerly lad with thick, reddish curls, given to hunting and shooting; facetious, teasing and careless. Later falls in love with the vicar of L——'s eldest daughter and exerts himself enormously to become worthy of her. Is given the family property when Gilbert marries and moves to his wife's estate. *The Tenant of Wildfell Hall*

MARKHAM, GILBERT: Elder son of a gentleman farmer destined by his father in spite of his own ambitions to farm in his turn. Initially attracted to the vicar's sly, piquant daughter Eliza Millward, he falls in love with the mysterious tenant of Wildfell Hall, Mrs. Helen Graham. Rumours that she is the mistress of his friend the local squire, Mr. Lawrence, soon seem confirmed by an overheard affectionate conversation and, disillusioned, he reproaches her so bitterly that she allows him to read her journal for the last six years. When he finds she is not widowed but escaping from a drunken, brutal husband, Arthur Huntingdon, and is Lawrence's sister, they are reconciled. When she returns to nurse her dying husband, Gilbert is stricken, rather than triumphant, at his death. Rumours of her remarriage send him in haste to her new home (where Lawrence, not she, is marrying), and a further setback, in the form of her large inheritance from her uncle, discourages him; but she dispels his diffidence and pride, and they marry. A countryman of no remarkable attainments or piety, his honesty and generosity form a strong enough contrast with the unreliable, disingenuous Arthur Huntingdon. *The Tenant of Wildfell Hall*

MARKHAM, ROSE: Sister of Gilbert Markham, a smart, pretty girl with a tidy dumpy figure, a round face, bright blooming cheeks, clustering curls and little merry brown eyes; a kind good-tempered girl equally disposed to befriend the village gossips and disbelieve their scandal. Sometimes complains of her mother's spoiling her brothers. Later marries Halford, recipient of Gilbert's story of Wildfell Hall. *The Tenant of Wildfell Hall*

MARTHA: Housekeeper to the implied author, compares the novel's setting before and after industrial development. *Shirley*

MARTHA: Mrs. Bretton's servant. *Villette*

MARY: Mr. Rochester's cook at Thornfield, married to John the coachman: they look after Rochester when, blind and maimed, he moves to Ferndean Manor. *Jane Eyre*

MARY: Servant at Thrushcross Grange, a thoughtless girl who brings the rumours of Isabella's elopement. *Wuthering Heights*

MASON, BERTHA ANTOINETTA: Mr. Rochester's mad wife. Daughter of Jonas Mason, a merchant in the West Indies, and Antoinetta his wife, a mad, drunken Créole, she is the boast of Spanish Town for her beauty when Rochester goes there as a young man. Their fathers, though aware of her mother's madness, plan their marriage to unite her wealth and his ancient name. Dazzled, Rochester marries her without knowing her character, which turns out to be low, and her violent temper and libertine propensities hasten the development of her insanity, which at this period precluded divorce. She is taken to England, where no one knows about the marriage, and secretly kept at Thornfield Hall attended by Grace Poole, where her presence but not her identity is suspected. Occasionally escapes from her room, once to set fire to Rochester's room, finally to burn down the house, perishing in the flames. Originally tall, dark and majestic like Blanche Ingram, she becomes bulky, swollen and empurpled in her insanity, a frightening incarnation of fleshly vice. *Jane Eyre*

MASON, JONAS: A rich merchant of Jamaica, father of Richard, Bertha and a younger son (a dumb idiot), friend of old Mr. Rochester, he agrees to give Bertha a fortune of thirty thousand pounds and marry her to Edward Rochester. *Jane Eyre*

MASON, ANTOINETTA: Wife of Jonas Mason, a Créole, a madwoman and drunkard, confined to an asylum. She has bequeathed her insanity to her children. *Jane Eyre*

MASON, RICHARD: Born in the West Indies, son of Jonas and Antoinetta Mason, brother of Mr. Rochester's mad wife Bertha. Though conventionally handsome with small regular features, his wandering, vacant gaze repels Jane

Eyre and Rochester prophesies that he too will become mad. He has however a mild, affectionate nature, was once attached to Rochester and still is very concerned for Bertha, this concern leading him rashly to visit her alone, whereupon she savagely attacks him with a knife and with her teeth. Meeting Jane Eyre's uncle back in the West Indies he hears of her proposed marriage to Rochester, reveals that this would be bigamy, and accompanies a lawyer to interrupt the wedding. *Jane Eyre*

MATHILDE DE ——: Heiress of a Belgian count, attends the school of Frances Crimsworth (née Henri) in Brussels. *The Professor*

MATHILDE: A pupil of Mme Beck. *Villette*

MATOU, ROSINE: Portress at Mme. Beck's school. A typical soubrette, her pert directness wins Lucy Snowe's rather patronising approval. As well as the brightness of her comments, she contributes a temporary and laboured mystification to the plot when Lucy suspects her—wrongly —of having fascinated Dr. John. *Villette*

MAXWELL, MR.: Husband of Helen Huntingdon's aunt, a kindly, bluff man afflicted by gout, who lets his niece marry whom she likes and leaves his property to her when he dies. *The Tenant of Wildfell Hall*

MAXWELL, MRS. PEGGY: Helen Huntingdon's aunt, a grave but kind woman, wishes her to marry a really good man and so disapproves of her suitor, the charming, selfish Mr. Huntingdon. Disappointed when they marry, she persuades her husband to leave his rich estate which had been her dowry to her niece. When both are widowed she lives with her, even after Helen's remarriage to Gilbert Markham (whom she approves), until she dies. *The Tenant of Wildfell Hall*

MELCY, BLANCHE DE: A baronne, pupil of Mme. Beck,

the eldest, tallest, handsomest and most vicious of her class. Tries to overthrow Lucy Snowe's first attempt at teaching; has her very stupid essay torn up. *Villette*

MELTHAM, HARRY: Younger son of Sir Hugh Meltham and therefore penniless and ineligible for Rosalie Murray, who rather prefers him. Flirts with her in London after her marriage, which is one reason for her husband's sending her to the country. *Agnes Grey*

MELTHAM, SIR HUGH: Attends Rosalie Murray's coming out ball, father of Harry, her favourite admirer. Always ignores the governess, Agnes Grey. Also LADY MELTHAM, MR. MELTHAM his eldest son, married and living in London, and MISS MELTHAM. *Agnes Grey*

MICHAEL: A groom at Thrushcross Grange, thinking of leaving to get married. He is fond of reading, and in return for gifts of books gets the younger Catherine's pony ready for her secret trips to visit Linton Heathcliff. *Wuthering Heights*

MILLER, MISS: An ordinary, ruddy-faced woman who looks what she is—an under-teacher at Lowood school. She has charge of Jane Eyre who shares her bed on the first night of her arrival. *Jane Eyre*

MILLWARD, ELIZA: Younger daughter of the vicar of Lindenhope, a very engaging little creature, with long narrow eyes, almost black, often both wicked and bewitching. Though penniless she attracts Gilbert Markham and is so resentful when he turns his attentions to Helen Huntingdon (Mrs. Graham) that she spares no malice to blacken her character or annoy him. Later marries a wealthy but dull tradesman and leads him an uncomfortable life. *The Tenant of Wildfell Hall*

MILLWARD, MARY: Daughter of the vicar of Lindenhope, several years older than her sister Eliza and of larger, coarser build. A plain, quiet, sensible girl, she acts as housekeeper and family drudge, never listens to scandal, and becomes secretly engaged to the studious Richard Wilson, whom she marries when he becomes her father's curate. *The Tenant of Wildfell Hall*

MILLWARD, THE REV. MICHAEL: Vicar of Lindenhope, a tall, ponderous, elderly gentleman of fixed principles, strong prejudices and regular habits, intolerant of dissent in every shape. He has a robust appetite for food and drink. Believes the scandal about Mrs. Graham. Eventually has to admit his large parish is too much for his energy, and takes on as his curate Richard Wilson, who succeeds him as vicar when he dies. *The Tenant of Wildfell Hall*

MINNIE: Maid to the Crimsworths in Brussels. *The Professor*

MIRET: A bookseller, supplying Mme. Beck's school. Bad-tempered in general but courteous to Lucy. Landlord of the school she eventually rents, to which he sends his three daughters. *Villette*

MOORE, GERARD: Father of Hortense, Louis and Robert. Inherits family business debts, which he bequeathes in turn to Robert. *Shirley*

MOORE, HORTENSE: Elder sister of Robert and Louis Moore, a good sister and excellent housekeeper, she has a high opinion of herself and her ways. Causes amusement by adhering to Flemish styles of dress and cookery. She teaches Caroline French, fine needlework and arithmetic. *Shirley*

MOORE, LOUIS GERARD: Brother of Robert and Hortense Moore, is sent to England in youth to learn English, later becomes an under-teacher, later still tutor to Henry Sympson, and also teaches Shirley Keeldar French. He and Shirley love one another but have to overcome their pride and the difference of their fortunes. Not as handsome or vital as his brother, Louis has a weightier, kinder character. His trials resemble Caroline's, but his strength and work support him. *Shirley*

MOORE, ROBERT GERARD: Caroline Helstone's cousin, would return her love but distracted by financial troubles. Master of a cloth mill, he is cut off from markets abroad by the Napoleonic wars. Blamed by the weavers for falling wages and his attempt to mechanise his mill, he defies machine-breakers and armed attacks. His overriding ambition seems less noble after his mercenary motives for proposing to Shirley are indignantly discovered, and he is almost killed by an assassin's bullet. He then decides to marry Caroline, even before peace saves him by reviving trade. An industrial version of the romantic hero, he has to learn that self-aggrandisement is at the expense of principle and other people's suffering. *Shirley*

MUHLER, HEINRICH: A blond young German merchant, engaged to M. Paul's goddaughter, Justine-Marie Sauveur. *Villette*

MULLENBERG, AMELIE: The eldest and most turbulent pupil of a group that Frances Henri cannot control. *The Professor*

MURGATROYD, FRED: Works at Robert Moore's mill, is tied up by machine-breakers. Discovers their leader was Barraclough, his rival for Moore's servant Sarah. *Shirley*

MURRAY, MR.: Husband of Mrs. Murray, a tall, stout gentleman with scarlet cheeks and a crimson nose, is seen by Agnes Grey occasionally, and is said to be a blustering, roistering country squire, a devoted foxhunter, a skilful horse-jockey and farrier, an active practical farmer and a hearty *bon vivant*. Obstinate self-indulgence leads to the gout, which makes him very ferocious. *Agnes Grey*

MURRAY, MRS.: Agnes Grey's second employer. A handsome, dashing lady of forty, in no need of rouge or padding to add to her charms, her chief enjoyments being parties and fashionable dressing. Indulgent towards her children, she can later exert her authority (in violent scenes) to compel at least Matilda to obedience. Is not unkind to Agnes, but condescending rather than considerate. *Agnes Grey*

MURRAY, CHARLES: Youngest of the Murray children and his mother's favourite. A puny, selfish, bad-tempered, malicious child of ten who can barely read, he has to have his lessons made easy by Agnes Grey and is never to be reprimanded, so that he goes to school in a state of disgraceful ignorance. Later is said to have become a fine, bold, unruly, mischievous boy. *Agnes Grey*

MURRAY, JOHN: Elder son of the Murrays, a fine, stout, healthy boy but rough as a young bear, and unteachable, at least by Agnes Grey. Is sent to school within a year. *Agnes Grey*

MURRAY, MATILDA: Younger daughter of the Murrays, a veritable hoyden, big-boned and awkward, but caring little about her appearance. Gallops and blunders through her lessons, but is happy as a lark riding or romping with the dogs: her virtue is honesty. Delicacy, however, is lacking, as witness her habit of swearing like a trooper, reprimanded in vain by Agnes Grey. Eventually, seeing that 'Tilly, though she would have made a fine lad, was not quite what a young lady ought to be', her parents exert their authority to tame her and after Agnes leaves a fashionable governess is reported to be improving her manners. *Agnes Grey*

MURRAY, ROSALIE: Elder daughter of the Murrays, who develops from a very pretty girl to a positive beauty, slender, exquisitely fair and blue-eyed. Lively and light-hearted but very vain, she comes to hold Agnes Grey in as much affection as is possible for her shallow nature. Though quick-brained, she cultivates only showy accomplishments and at seventeen and eighteen, ambitions to dazzle the opposite sex override all else. Approving her mother's plans to marry her to the wicked, ugly but rich Sir Thomas Ashby ('for I *must* have Ashby Park whoever shares it with me') she purposely sets out to attract the vicar, Mr. Hatfield, so that she can mortify him by refusing to marry him, and likewise tries to entangle the curate Mr. Weston, to the unhappiness of Agnes Grey who loves him. After her marriage her flirtatiousness and extravagance cause her husband to keep her away from London at Ashby Park, where she comes to detest him enough to enjoy even a visit from Agnes. She has a baby daughter, whom she regards with no remarkable degree of interest or affection, and though recompensed for her mercenary heartlessness, she is sadder but no wiser. *Agnes Grey*

MYERS, MISS ALICE: Arthur Huntingdon's mistress, introduced into his home as governess to his son. Has few accomplishments except a fine voice, and has a look of guilt and subtlety that arouses Helen Huntingdon's suspicions. Leaves him before his fatal illness. *The Tenant of Wildfell Hall*

N

NASMYTH, THE REV.: A clergyman, an excellent man, almost worthy of Lowood's headmistress Miss Temple, whom he marries and takes to a distant country. *Jane Eyre*

NOAH O'TIM'S: Self-satisfied though not dishonest second-in-command in Barraclough's deputation; he rhetorically advises Robert Moore to leave England. *Shirley*

NUNNELY, SIR PHILIP: Owns Nunnely Priory and is the only baronet in the area. Slight, boyish, sandy-haired, he is sensible, sensitive and kind—but infatuated with his own very bad verse. Proposes marriage to Shirley Keeldar, is refused. *Shirley*

NUNNELY, LADY: Mother of Sir Philip, disapproves of Shirley. Also, NUNNELY, the MISSES: Her daughters, pattern young ladies, look askance at Shirley's unconventionality. *Shirley*

O

O'GALL, MRS. DIONYSIUS: Of Bitternutt Lodge, Connaught, Ireland, with five daughters. A fictional character invented by Rochester as a prospective employer for Jane Eyre when he rather cruelly teases her as a preliminary to proposing marriage. *Jane Eyre*

OLDFIELD, MR.: The old, ugly, rich suitor found for Esther Hargrave, whom she refuses. He persists nevertheless. *The Tenant of Wildfell Hall*

OLIVER, MR. (BILL): A tall massive-featured, middle-aged and grey-headed man, owner of a needle factory and of Vale Hall in Morton Vale, though his father has been a journeyman needlemaker. Appears a taciturn and perhaps a proud person but is very kind to Jane Eyre, when a poor schoolmistress. Father of the beautiful Rosamond, he would like her to marry St. John Rivers who is of good though poor family. *Jane Eyre*

OLIVER, ROSAMOND: Daughter of Mr. Oliver the rich mill owner. Endowed with perfect beauty she has a direct and naïve simplicity, pleasing but childlike. She loves St. John Rivers who also loves her, but he renounces her and her wealth ('Rose of the World' as her name signifies), being dedicated to missionary work in India. Easily consoled, however, she soon marries the rich Mr. Granby. Coquettish but not heartless, she is neither as original as the Rivers sisters nor as snobbish and affected as the Ingrams: Jane Eyre classes her with Adèle Varens as likeable but 'not profoundly interesting'. *Jane Eyre*

P

PANACHE, MME.: A bellicose history teacher at Mme. Beck's school, provokes M. Paul's wholehearted irritation and enmity. Once dismissed and impoverished, she is pitied and helped by him, but immediately rouses his antipathy again when they next meet face to face. *Villette*

PATH, LOUISE: A country-bred pupil of Mlle. Reuter, she possesses the happiest disposition in the school. Benevolent and obliging, she is however ill-mannered and not completely honest. *The Professor*

PEARSON, MR.: A mill owner, prevented from selling cloth to America by the wartime 'Orders in Council'. Is shot at through his staircase window. *Shirley*

PEARSON, ANNE: Daughter of Mr. Pearson, a mature young lady whose name has been coupled with Robert Moore's. Also, KATE and SUSAN, probably her younger sisters, friends of Rose and Jessie Yorke. *Shirley*

PELAGIE and SUZETTE, MLLES.: French teachers at Mlle. Reuter's school, ordinary in looks, manner, temper, thoughts, feelings and views. *The Professor*

PELET, FRANÇOIS: Headmaster of a boys' school where he employs William Crimsworth to teach English and Latin.

Is engaged to Zoraïde Reuter, headmistress of the girls' school next door, but conceals this from Crimsworth whose feelings towards her he wishes to investigate. Becomes jealous later, but is conciliated by Zoraïde and regains affability and complacency when they marry. An intelligent, suave Frenchman, he is generally friendly towards Crimsworth, and tactfully avoids shocking him with tales of his amatory exploits. *The Professor*

PELET, MME.: M. Pelet's mother, a coarse, jolly old Frenchwoman who acts as housekeeper in his school. Approached by Mme. Reuter, her friend and opposite number, she sounds out William Crimsworth's willingness to give lessons in the girls' school next door. *The Professor*

PIERROT, MME.: Elderly French teacher at Lowood school; wears a handkerchief tied to her side by a yellow riband and displeases the child Jane Eyre because she is harsh and grotesque. *Jane Eyre*

PIGHILLS, JEREMIAH: Works at Moore's mill, later said by Martin Yorke to be a sweetheart of Moore's servant Sarah. *Shirley*

PILLULE, DR.: Former doctor to Mme. Beck's school, supplanted by Dr. John Bretton. *Villette*

POOLE, GRACE: Ostensibly hired to sew and assist generally at Thornfield Hall, she is really, as servants and neighbours guess, the keeper of the madwoman concealed there. Formerly employed at the Grimsby Retreat asylum, experienced and very discreet, she is one of the few to know the madwoman is really Rochester's legal wife. Having a professional weakness for drink, she sometimes lets her charge escape, which eventually leads to the burning down of the Hall. A woman of between thirty and forty, with a set square-made figure, red hair and a hard plain face, she defies Jane Eyre's conjectures. Has a son, also a keeper at the Grimsby Retreat. *Jane Eyre*

PROFESSOR, THE: *see* Crimsworth, William

PRYOR, MRS.: Shirley's companion, formerly her governess. Real name Agnes Helstone, née Grey, she is Caroline Helstone's mother, but escapes from her drunken husband, the sadistic James. For fear Caroline has inherited her father's vices with his appearance, she consigns her to the Rev. Mr. Helstone. Reveals her identity in time to restore Caroline's will to live during her serious illness. A High Tory, she deprecates change and advocates deference to superiors. Is so shy and ill-assured she is generally misunderstood and disliked. *Shirley*

R

RACHEL: Helen Huntingdon's lady's maid, once her nurse, later nurses her son Arthur. A faithful, taciturn, respectable woman who loves Helen and hates her husband enough to accompany her on her secret flight, afterwards working as her general servant for low wages; she even offers Helen her own savings. *The Tenant of Wildfell Hall*

RAMSDEN, TIMOTHY: Stout corn-factor of Royd Mill; harrassed by Shirley out of his chair which she intends for Robert Moore at the Whitsuntide gathering. *Shirley*

RAMSDEN, MRS.: Has ordered some children's socks from the charity 'Jew Basket' which Caroline Helstone has to knit. *Shirley*

REED, ELIZA: Elder daughter of Mrs. Reed and Jane Eyre's cousin. Grows from a sharp, selfish child, who 'would have sold the hair off her head if she could have made a handsome profit thereby', into a thin, pallid, ascetic woman. She is as rigid a formalist in religion as she is in fulfilling a self-imposed daily ritual of duties. After her mother's death she studies Roman Catholicism, then becomes a nun and eventually mother superior in a French convent. Approves Jane for the qualities they have in common—rationality and self-sufficiency—but is quite devoid of 'true generous feeling'. *Jane Eyre*

REED, GEORGIANA: Mrs. Reed's younger daughter. Grows from a spoiled, spiteful but sweetly pretty child into a full-blown plump damsel, fair as a waxwork. A social success in London, she is foiled by her sister's betrayal in her plans to elope with a titled admirer. Ignoring her mother's illness and brother's suicide, she longs only to re-enter society. Finally makes an advantageous match with a wealthy, worn-out man of fashion. As selfish as her sister, she has much superficial sentimentality but no judgment at all. *Jane Eyre*

REED, JOHN: Mrs. Reed's son, her favourite. As a large, stout, unwholesome, flabby boy of fourteen he violently bullies Jane Eyre his cousin, and her retaliation is punished by imprisonment in the haunted Red Room. Grows into a tall, thick-lipped young man, ruins his health and estate among the worst men and worst women, gets into debt and into jail. Failing finally to extract more money from his mother, he commits suicide. This provokes Mrs. Reed's fatal apoplectic stroke. *Jane Eyre*

REED, MRS. SARAH: Née Gibson. Jane Eyre's aunt, who resents her husband's fondness for his sister and his taking in her orphaned daughter Jane. A woman of robust frame, with prominent jaw and eyes devoid of ruth, she is equally devoid of ruth in bringing up Jane after her husband's death, for like her children she has little genuine feeling, though she dotes on them. Shaken by Jane's passionate self-justification she sends her to school, and later falsely tells John Eyre, her uncle, that she died of typhus there, wishing to prevent any inheritance coming to Jane. After the degeneration, debt and suicide of her favourite child John, she suffers an apoplectic stroke, but confesses her lie to Jane on her deathbed. *Jane Eyre*

REUTER, MME.: Mlle. Reuter's mother, acts as housekeeper in her daughter's school, but resembles a joyous, free-living old Flemish farmer's wife. Approaches William Crimsworth through her friend and opposite number Mme. Pelet as to his giving English lessons at the girls' school. *The Professor*

REUTER, ZORAÏDE: Headmistress of a girls' school, next door to M. Pelet's. Employs William Crimsworth to give additional English lessons. She tries to attract him, partly to gain a hold over him, and has some initial success, but when he is disillusioned by overhearing her conversation with Pelet, secretly her fiancé, she in turn becomes infatuated by his disdain, to the point almost of losing Pelet. Jealousy causes her to dismiss her Anglo-Swiss needlework teacher, Frances Henri, and conceal her address from Crimsworth who thereupon resigns his post. She then regains self-control, conciliates and marries Pelet. Her infatuation and attractions are such however that Crimsworth foresees intrigue and leaves Pelet's house and employment. Rational and cunning, she manages everything by indirect means, and though intelligent she lacks integrity and sensitivity, and has none of Frances Henri's originality and enthusiasm. *The Professor*

RICHARD: Arthur Huntingdon's coachman. *The Tenant of Wildfell Hall*

RICHARDSON, MR.: A clergyman, marries Mary Grey, Agnes' sister. A good, wise, amiable man of thirty-six or -seven, not rich—only comfortable; not handsome—only decent; and not young—only middling. *Agnes Grey*

RILE, DR.: Attends Caroline Helstone, gives non-committal advice with an air of crushing authority. *Shirley*

RIVERS, DIANA: Sister of Mary and St. John, cousin of Jane Eyre, whom she and her sister take in when starving, without knowing their relationship. Tall with long dark curls, she has a strong character and dominates her sister and cousin; she is as strong-willed as her brother. Works as a governess after her late father's bankruptcy, until Jane makes over to her a portion of their common uncle's legacy. Marries Captain Fitzjames. *Jane Eyre*

RIVERS, MARY: Sister of Diana and St. John. Wears her light brown hair in smooth braids, is milder and gentler than her sister, and undemonstrative sincerity is characteristic of her. A governess until given a portion of Jane Eyre's legacy, she marries a clergyman, Mr. Wharton. *Jane Eyre*

RIVERS (OLD) MR.: Father of St. John, Diana and Mary, a plain enough man 'stark mad o' shooting and farming and sich like', but of a family notable 'i' th'owd days o' the Henrys'. Loses his money by trusting a man who goes bankrupt, so his daughters have to become governesses. His children are at home for his funeral when Jane Eyre meets them. Also his wife, a more cultivated lady, whose studious habits have been inherited by their children. *Jane Eyre*

RIVERS, ST. JOHN: Descendant of an old but impoverished family, clergyman at Morton, brother of Diana and Mary and cousin of Jane Eyre. Not knowing Jane's identity he takes her in when she collapses on his sisters' doorstep and later finds her work as village schoolmistress. Spiritually ambitious, he plans to follow his vocation as a missionary and therefore suppresses his love for the beautiful but frivolous heiress Rosamond Oliver. Tries to persuade Jane, a much more suitable missionary's wife, to marry him instead, and though bitterly offended by her denunciation of loveless marriage, he is thwarted only by Rochester's strange telepathic summons to Jane and her subsequent flight. Goes to India alone and prepares to die there. Gifted with terrifying self-control, he does not value earthly happiness: as beautiful as a marble statue in appearance, he tries to become as marble to the passions too. *Jane Eyre*

ROAKES: A mill owner, prevented from selling cloth to America by the war-time 'Orders in Council'. *Shirley*

ROBERT: A groom or coachman at Horton Lodge, whose society Matilda Murray prefers to her governess's. *Agnes Grey*

ROBERT: Old Mr. Linton's servant, sets the bulldog on Catherine Earnshaw and Heathcliff, straying in Thrushcross Grange grounds. *Wuthering Heights*

ROCHEMORT: *see* Boissec and Rochemort

ROCHESTER, MR.: Father of Edward Fairfax Rochester, a grasping proud man, whose avariciousness makes him unwilling to divide the inheritance of his elder son, but whose pride equally deters him from seeing his younger son Edward impoverished. Therefore he causes Edward to marry Bertha Mason, the rich daughter of an old West Indian acquaintance, though aware of hereditary insanity in her family. When this insanity appears in Bertha, however, he shares his son's anxiety to conceal the marriage. Dies nine years before Jane Eyre comes to Thornfield. *Jane Eyre*

ROCHESTER, DAMER DE: An ancestor of Edward Rochester, slain at Marston Moor in the civil wars, buried in a time-stained marble tomb in Hay church. Also, ELIZABETH, his wife, buried with him. *Jane Eyre*

ROCHESTER, EDWARD FAIRFAX: The younger son of an ambitious man, he is provided for by an arranged marriage (endorsed by her purely physical attractions) with Bertha Mason, heiress of a West Indian merchant, who later turns out to be mad, which by the law of the period precludes divorce. He inherits Thornfield and, concealing his marriage, shuts up his wife there secretly with a keeper. After being involved with a succession of mistresses in Europe, he returns to Thornfield where Jane Eyre is the governess of his ward, Adèle Varens. He then attempts to marry Jane, arguing that his first marriage is morally void, and when this is foiled by Bertha's brother, presses her to become his mistress. After she secretly leaves Thornfield, the house is burnt down by the madwoman, who dies in the flames. Rochester, trying to save her, loses a hand and his sight, which he regards as punishment for wishing to 'sully my Innocent Flower'. A recluse at Ferndean Manor, his calls for Jane are supernaturally communicated to her: she rejoins him, they marry, and have a son, Edward. He partially recovers his sight. Dark, powerfully built and with harsh strong features that are unattractive to his conventional young lady guests, he is abrupt in manner and though intelligent, dangerously subject to his passions: his thoughtless infatuation with Bertha Mason's beauty is as blameworthy as his father's mercenary plot for all his subsequent misery. *Jane Eyre*

ROCHESTER, ROWLAND: Elder brother of Edward Rochester, destined by his father to inherit the whole family fortune, entirely excluding his younger brother (with whom, moreover, he has many misunderstandings). Plans with his father to marry Edward to the heiress Bertha Mason, though aware of her family history of insanity. Dies before his father. *Jane Eyre*

ROGERS, HANNAH: A Horton villager who wants Nancy Browne to help her wash, and finding her unprepared, begins scolding, but her wrath is turned away by a soft answer, as advised by the curate. *Agnes Grey*

ROSALIE: Portress at Mlle. Reuter's school. *The Professor*

ROUSE, MRS.: A member of the 'Jew Basket' rota. *Shirley*

RUTH: A servant of the young Miss Marchmont. *Villette*

RYDE, COLONEL: In charge of the barracks where Robert Moore procures soldiers to defend his mill. *Shirley*

S

ST. PIERRE, ZELIE DE: A Parisian teacher at Mme. Beck's School, is snubbed when she offers friendship and confides her libertine tendencies to Lucy, and thereafter hates her. 'Cold and snaky' but well-dressed, she hopes to attract Paul Emanuel. *Villette*

SALLY: Maid to Agnes Grey's family, initially one of two, she alone is retained after their impoverishment, though the less efficient (being the less expensive). *Agnes Grey*

SAM: Footman at Thornfield Hall, announces the arrival of the supposed gipsy fortune-teller (really Mr. Rochester in disguise) to the house party, and attempting to warn the ladies, is dismissed by Blanche Ingram in the immortal words 'Cease thy chatter, blockhead! and do my bidding'. *Jane Eyre*

SARA, LADY: Daughter of an English peer, an honest though haughty-looking girl, accompanies Ginevra to the concert but behaves more modestly. *Villette*

SARAH: Mrs. Reed's housemaid. After Jane Eyre faints in the haunted room, she is summoned by Bessie the nurse-maid to keep her company, and they spend the evening telling ghost stories, which far from reassures the terrified Jane. *Jane Eyre*

SARAH: Robert and Hortense Moore's pretty, independent

servant. Keeps up a running battle against her mistress's Flemish ways, and attracts various suitors. *Shirley*

SARAH: Maid to the Millwards, who carries gossip to Eliza Millward. *The Tenant of Wildfell Hall*

SAUVEUR, JUSTINE-MARIE: A handsome heiress, the 18-year-old goddaughter of Paul Emanuel, niece of his dead fiancée Justine-Marie. An unfounded and improbable plan to marry her to M. Paul is overheard by Lucy Snowe. Is in fact engaged to Heinrich Muhler. *Villette*

SCATCHERD, MISS: A small, dark, smart but morose upper teacher of history and grammar at Lowood school. Her bad temper leads her to victimise the intellectual, pious Helen Burns for her untidiness. It is the caning which she administers to her that gives Helen the opportunity of correcting Jane Eyre's vicarious indignation. A materialist who is blinded to spiritual worth by superficial imperfections. *Jane Eyre*

SCOTT, HARRY: Joe Scott's son, who hangs about Moore's mill all day. Carries messages, etc. *Shirley*

SCOTT, JOE: 'Overlooker' at Robert Moore's mill. An example of 'us manufacturing lads in the north', he is sharp-witted, frank and well-informed, qualities he perhaps over-estimates. Without impertinence, he tells Shirley and Caroline that politics are above young ladies' heads. *Shirley*

SEACOMBE, THE HON. JOHN: Brother of the Crimsworths' mother, whom, like Lord Tynedale, he disowns after his misalliance and refuses to aid during her destitute widowhood. Hints that William Crimsworth may marry one of his daughters if he enters the Church—this offer is rejected. *The Professor*

SEACOMBE, SARAH: One of the six daughters of John

Seacombe, William Crimsworth's uncle, a large and well-modelled statue whom he cannot bear to consider as a wife. *The Professor*

SEVERN, JULIA: A pupil at Lowood school: instead of being combed straight back her red hair curls naturally and so rouses Mr. Brocklehurst's wrath; he does not believe in conforming to nature and orders her and all other pupils with thick hair to have it cut off. *Jane Eyre*

SILAS, PERE: A French Jesuit priest of about seventy, he hears Lucy's 'confession' and hopes to convert her to Catholicism. Has been Paul Emanuel's tutor and is now partly supported by him, and influences him against marrying the Protestant Lucy. In spite of his deviousness he is basically kind, sincere and intelligent. *Villette*

SMITH, MISS: A red-cheeked teacher at Lowood school, teaches all kinds of needlework and supervises the pupils' clothing. *Jane Eyre*

SMITH, MR.: The draper, grocer and tea-dealer of the village where Agnes' father Richard Grey runs up a bill while waiting to make a large fortune by trade. He and his gig are hired to drive Agnes to her first employers' house. *Agnes Grey*

SNOWE, LUCY: After early financial misfortune she works as a companion to the invalid Miss Marchmont, then goes abroad to Labassecour where she is hired as nursemaid by a headmistress, Mme. Beck, and later promoted to English teacher. Becoming depressed and ill in the lonely vacation, she seeks relief (though a Protestant) in the confessional, collapsing afterwards in the street. Taken home by Dr. John, whose mother is recognised as her godmother, she recovers. Her suppressed attraction for Dr. John is put aside just as Professor Paul Emanuel's interest in her becomes apparent. His relations part them for religious and financial reasons, but before he is sent abroad he rents a tiny school for her, in which she waits for him—his return is left doubtful. Philosophical and cold in girlhood, Lucy later believes herself destined to exceptional suffering. On the one hand a prey to morbid depression, she steels herself to endure patiently; on the other she is stimulated by work and her powerful imagination. Hence many consider her grave or even cynical, whereas M. Paul finds her passionate and hasty. *Villette*

SOMEBODY, CAPTAIN, AND LIEUTENANT SOMETHING ELSE: Two military fops, visitors to the Greens, who walk back from church with them and the Miss Murrays. *Agnes Grey*

SOPHIE: The French nursemaid who accompanies Mr. Rochester's ward, Adèle Varens, to England. Speaking no English she can talk only to Adèle until Jane Eyre arrives as governess. Not being of a descriptive or narrative turn, she is not a mine of information about France, but is a pleasant, respectable girl. *Jane Eyre*

STAAS, M. LE CHEVALIER: A Villette worthy, attends the oration at the Athénée prize-giving. *Villette*

STEIGHTON, TIMOTHY: Edward Crimsworth's first clerk, a man of about thirty-five with a face at once sly and heavy; a 'joined Methodist' and an ingrained rascal, spies on William Crimsworth for his master. *The Professor*

SUGDEN: A constable, summoned by Robert Moore to arrest Barraclough as a machine-breaker. *Shirley*

SUMNER, MR.: Schoolmaster at the grammar school. *Shirley*

SUPPLEHOUGH: A dissenting preacher. More hardworking than the curates, he wins many converts. *Shirley*

SUZETTE: *see* Pélagie and Suzette, Mlles.

SVINI, MME.: see Sweeny

SWEENY, MME. (or SVINI): Lucy's predecessor as nurse-maid to Mme. Beck's children, she is Irish, and dresses in showy handed-down clothes. Coarse and a drunkard, she keeps her post a month by virtue of her status symbol, a 'real Indian shawl'. *Villette*

SWEETING, DAVID: Curate of Nunnely. A little, good-natured ladies' man, he is unimpressive but not ridiculous. Plays the flute. Eventually marries Dora, the largest Miss Sykes. *Shirley*

SYKES, CHRISTOPHER: A mill owner, comely but weak. Nervous of the weavers' deputation, he is emboldened by Hollands gin. *Shirley*

SYKES, MRS.: A kindly, matchmaking woman. *Shirley*

SYKES, THE MISSES: Supposedly six, only four appear. DORA: tall, handsome, the stoutest, is good-natured and eventually marries Sweeting. HANNAH: dashing, pushing and empty-headed enough to tempt Mr. Helstone. HARRIET: tall, handsome, the beauty—expects homage. MARY: well-disposed, the most sensible. All very self-possessed. *Shirley*

SYKES, JOHN: Son of Christopher. *Shirley*

SYKES: Works at Moore's mill. *Shirley*

SYLVIE: A pale, ugly, stunted pupil of Mlle. Reuter, destined to be a nun. With intelligence, modesty and application worthy of Frances Henri's, she has nevertheless been 'warped to a conventual bias'—her will is sapped and her profound religious submissiveness has made her an automaton, a result as harmful as the low moral standards of the pupils who pay only lip-service to their religion. *The Professor*

SYMPSON, MR.: Shirley's uncle. A man of spotless

respectability, worrying temper, pious principles and worldly views. Tries unavailingly to influence Shirley's marital plans. *Shirley*

SYMPSON, MRS.: A very good woman, patient and kind but dreadfully narrow-minded. Outwardly submissive, really rules her husband. Also SYMPSON, THE MISSES GERTRUDE and ISABELLA: an example to their sex, they condemn any deviations from their pattern of behaviour. *Shirley*

SYMPSON, HENRY (HARRY): Shirley's favourite cousin, son of Mr. Sympson, a little, lame pale boy of fifteen, 'desperately fond' of Shirley. *Shirley*

T

TEMPLE, MISS MARIA: Superintendent (headmistress) of Lowood school, dark-haired, tall and shapely, she is far more stately and refined than the other teachers. Deplores but does not openly criticise the meanness of the school treasurer, Mr. Brocklehurst, and investigates fairly his description of Jane Eyre's character as deceitful. As mild and disciplined in character as her favourite, the consumptive Helen Burns, she influences Jane, to whom she becomes mother, governess and companion, with her own tranquillity. This influence is removed when she marries a clergyman, Mr. Nasmyth, and moves far away. By their justice, serenity and piety, she and Helen personify the beneficial effects of Lowood's austerity on Jane, changing her from a rebellious child into a self-contained young woman. *Jane Eyre*

THOMAS (TOM): Mr. Helstone's clerk and assistant. *Shirley*

THOMAS: Manservant of the Maxwells. *The Tenant of Wildfell Hall*

THOMAS: A servant of the young Miss Marchmont. *Villette*

TRINETTE: Maid to the Beck children. *Villette*

TRISTA, JOANNA: A Belgian-Spanish pupil of Mlle. Reuter. Dark of hair and gaunt of face, she disturbs lessons by snorting and spitting, and is quelled by being locked in a cabinet. Returns abroad, rejoicing in the prospect of ill-treating her slaves there. *The Professor*

TURNER, MISS: A poor, friendless, English teacher employed by Mme. Beck then dismissed for inability to control her boisterous class. *Villette*

TYNEDALE, LORD: Brother of Crimsworths' mother, whom he casts off after her misalliance and refuses to aid in her destitute widowhood. Pays for William Crimsworth's education at Eton (under pressure) and offers him a rich living in his gift if he enters the Church: this is refused. *The Professor*

V

VANDAM: *see* Kint and Vandam

VANDENHUTEN, JEAN BAPTISTE: A most ponderous young pupil of M. Pelet, who during an excursion capsizes a rowing boat and is rescued by William Crimsworth, who gains the gratitude and practical assistance of his parents. *The Professor*

VANDENHUTEN, VICTOR: Father of Jean Baptiste. A rich, respected and influential business-man of Brussels, who, because William Crimsworth saves his son from drowning, finds him work at a large boys' school. His good offices are not as burdensome as those of the clever but heartless Pelet: Crimsworth values his good-nature though slow and deliberate, thinking 'the benevolence of his truthful face was better than the intelligence of my own'. Also, VANDENHUTEN, MME.: his wife, especially touched by Crimsworth's rescue of her son. *The Professor*

VANDERKELHOV, JULES: A moon-faced Flemish pupil at M. Pelet's school who snuffles, snorts and wheezes through an English reading at William Crimsworth's first lesson. *The Professor*

VARENS, ADÈLE: Mr. Rochester's ward, whose governess Jane Eyre becomes, claimed to be his natural daughter, though there is no resemblance, by her mother Céline Varens, his mistress for some years. Abandoned when Céline elopes with a singer or actor, she is first kept by the kind but poor Mme. Frédéric, then is brought by Rochester 'to grow up clean in the wholesome soil of an English country garden'. Affectionate towards Jane, though shallow and with an innate devotion to dress, by the end of the novel 'a sound English education' has 'corrected in a great measure her French defects'. *Jane Eyre*

VARENS, CÉLINE: A French opera dancer, once Mr. Rochester's mistress. Professes to adore him but is caught out in infidelity and insincerity, which results in a duel between old and new lovers. Attributes the paternity of her daughter Adèle to Rochester. Abandoning her, she elopes to Italy with a musician or singer. *Jane Eyre*

VASHTI: Celebrated actress: 'upon her something neither of woman nor of man: in each of her eyes sat a devil.' The epitome of passion, her performance precedes a fire panic in the theatre. *Villette*

VERE, LORD EDWIN: A nobleman who is said to have loved Georgiana Reed, against the wishes of his family. Their planned elopement is betrayed by her sister Eliza Reed. *Jane Eyre*

VINING, MR.: A tutor once employed to teach Lord Ingram: a whey-faced would-be parson, he is suspected of falling in love with the Miss Ingrams' governess Miss Wilson, and is therefore dismissed. *Jane Eyre*

VIRGINIE: A titled pupil of Mme. Beck; sits with Blanche de Melcy. *Villette*

VOSS BROTHERS: A German firm whose correspondence William Crimsworth translates at work. *The Professor*

W

WADDY, SAM: A guest at Edward Crimsworth's birthday dance, he 'makes up' to a local belle, and is 'cut out' by the enterprising Yorke Hunsden. *The Professor*

WALRAVENS, MME. MAGLOIRE: A widow of nearly ninety, she is supported by Paul Emanuel for the sake of her dead granddaughter Justine-Marie, his fiancée, whose memory is the romantic trapping hiding the ugly reality of her exploitation (Mme. Walravens is 'hunchback, dwarfish and doting'), encouraged by his Church and selfish family. *Villette*

WARREN: Mrs. Bretton's servant. *Villette*

WATSONS, THE: Rich travellers on the Channel ferry, including a very young, beautiful girl married to the oldest, plainest, greasiest, broadest man. *Villette*

WESTON, EDWARD: Curate to Mr. Hatfield at Horton. Not handsome but decisive and striking in appearance, he is a man of strong sense, firm faith and ardent piety, thoughtful and stern but also kind and considerate. His taciturnity conceals his feelings towards Agnes Grey, whose hopes are dashed when her beautiful pupil Rosalie Murray tries to add him to her conquests. Apparently unaffected, however, he keeps informed of Agnes' departure to teach in her mother's school at A——, and later, when his quiet benevolence among the poor leads to dissension with Mr. Hatfield, he leaves to become vicar of F——, near her new home. They marry and have three children, EDWARD, AGNES and MARY. By his strenuous exertions he works surprising reforms in his new parish. *Agnes Grey*

WHARTON, MR.: A clergyman, college friend of St. John Rivers, of worthy principles and attainments, marries Mary Rivers. *Jane Eyre*

WHARTON, MRS.: An Englishwoman, living in Brussels, who employs Frances Henri to mend lace, discovers her history and obtains a post for her as French teacher in an English school in Brussels. *The Professor*

WHARTON, MISS: Daughter of Mrs. Wharton, she is about to be married and has received as wedding present the antique lace veil that Frances Henri mends. *The Professor*

WHIPP, MRS.: Mr. Sweeting's exasperated landlady. *Shirley*

WILLIAMSON: Servant of the Murrays, probably the lady's maid. *Agnes Grey*

WILMOT: Lucy's uncle. *Villette*

WILMOT, MR.: A rich old friend of Helen Huntingdon's uncle, disagreeable, ugly and wicked. He courts Helen against all discouragement and stops only when she marries Huntingdon. *The Tenant of Wildfell Hall*

WILMOT, ANNABELLA: Niece of the rich Mr. Wilmot, and an heiress in her own right, a fine dashing girl of five and twenty, dark, beautiful, flirtatious and a fine singer. Marries Lord Lowborough for his title, later becomes Arthur Huntingdon's mistress for over two years. Has two children, the younger, Annabella, not her husband's.

Afterwards elopes with another gallant to the continent, is divorced by her husband, goes dashing on for a season then sinks into debt and misery and is said to have died in utter wretchedness. *The Tenant of Wildfell Hall*

WILSON, MR.: The English teacher whom Lucy replaces. *Villette*

WILSON, MISS: Once governess to Blanche and Mary Ingram, a poor sickly thing, lachrymose and low-spirited, she falls in love with their brother's tutor Mr. Vining, and on suspicion of this is dismissed. *Jane Eyre*

WILSON, SIR BROADLEY: Attends Rosalie Murray's coming-out ball but is 'an old codger'. *Agnes Grey*

WILSON, MARY ANN: Pupil at Lowood school and friend of Jane Eyre. A shrewd observant personage, she likes to gossip and does not criticise. Her turn for narrative complements Jane's love of analysis; she contrasts with the serious Helen Burns who meanwhile is dying of consumption. *Jane Eyre*

WILSON, MRS.: Widow of a substantial farmer, mother of Robert, Richard and Jane, a narrow-minded, tattling old gossip. *The Tenant of Wildfell Hall*

WILSON, JANE: A young lady of some talents and more ambition, about six and twenty, with bright red hair, thin lips and clear hazel eyes devoid of poetry or feeling. Acquiring the polish of a boardschool education she wishes to marry a rich gentleman and aims at Frederick Lawrence. Gilbert Markham, resenting her supercilious malice against Helen Huntingdon, warns him of her selfishness and shallowness, so she remains unmarried, takes lodgings in the county town and lives in close-fisted, uncomfortable gentility. *The Tenant of Wildfell Hall*

WILSON, RICHARD: Younger son of Mrs. Wilson, a pale

quiet bookworm, he reads classics at Cambridge. Becomes secretly engaged to the vicar's plain elder daughter Mary, and when he becomes curate they marry. Later succeeds his father-in-law as vicar of Lindenhope. *The Tenant of Wildfell Hall*

WILSON, ROBERT: Elder son of Mrs. Wilson, a rough countrified farmer. When he marries, his proud sister Jane leaves the house. *The Tenant of Wildfell Hall*

WOOD, MR.: Clergyman at Hay Church near Thornfield, officiates at Rochester's interrupted wedding and is stopped by the production of a 'just cause or impediment'. Is taken to witness the madness of Rochester's first wife. *Jane Eyre*

WOOD, ALICE: A young orphan girl of Moreton, teachable and handy, who serves Jane Eyre as 'handmaid' at her cottage. *Jane Eyre*

WOOD, MARK: A poor labourer of Horton who is in the last stages of consumption, and tells Agnes Grey of the curate Mr. Weston's comfort and generosity, being 'another-guess sort of man' from the vicar Mr. Hatfield, whose attitude is inconsiderate and offensive. Agnes is sent to visit him by Rosalie Murray who wishes to be alone to flirt with Hatfield. Also his wife, who seems to call him Jem. *Agnes Grey*

WYNNE, MR.: A magistrate, owner of De Walden Hall. *Shirley*

WYNNE, SAMUEL FAWTHROP: Son and heir of Mr. Wynne, proposes marriage to Shirley, and is rejected on grounds of incompatibility, profligacy, vulgarity and stupidity. *Shirley*

WYNNE, THE MISSES: The two superlative daughters of Mr. Wynne, one light, one dark, their names are linked with Robert Moore's. *Shirley*

Y

YORKE, HIRAM: A proud republican of an old family, well-travelled, well-read, he varies his 'very pure English' with 'broad Yorkshire', being typically northern in his shrewd no-nonsense bluntness. His pride takes the form of attacking the established hierarchy, unlike the equally blunt Mr. Helstone, whom he delights to provoke (partly for political reasons, partly because he once loved Mary Cave who married Helstone). *Shirley*

YORKE, MRS. HESTHER: A large, portentous woman, strong-minded, cynical but a good wife and mother. Despises weakness, merriment and sentiment especially in young women. Ponderously hysterical when her children cross her, she rises with gusto to a real emergency like nursing Robert Moore. Has five older children and a baby. *Shirley*

YORKE, JESSIE: Younger daughter of Mr. Yorke. Piquant and pert, her father's pet, she is destined to die young. *Shirley*

YORKE, MARK: Middle son of Mr. Yorke. A bonnie-looking boy, but too phlegmatic: he is fourteen but his soul is thirty. *Shirley*

YORKE, MARTIN: Lively and independent younger son of Mr. Yorke. In spite of professing contempt for Caroline Helstone, he develops a precocious affection for her. Schemes for her to enter Robert Moore's well-defended sickroom at Briarmains, but is too diffident to ask a kiss as a reward. *Shirley*

YORKE, MATTHEW: Eldest son of Mr. Yorke. Handsome and independent, he has a violent, domineering temperament, exacerbated by his parents' conciliation. *Shirley*

YORKE, ROSE: Elder daughter of Mr. Yorke. A reserved, very thoughtful girl, is obedient but intends to be independent. After the novel ends travels in Europe where Jessie dies in her arms, then goes to the other side of the world. *Shirley*

Z

ZEPHYRINE, MLLE.: French teacher at Mlle. Reuter's school. A genuine Parisienne coquette, perfidious, mercenary and dry-hearted. *The Professor*

ZILLAH: Housekeeper at Wuthering Heights, taken on while Linton Heathcliff is still alive. A narrow-minded, selfish woman, she is offended by young Catherine and gives her no sympathy or help. Saves Lockwood from the dogs' attack, and leaves the Heights soon after this. *Wuthering Heights*

Z——, M.: A very learned but quiet courtly Frenchman, who talks to Paulina Mary Home while dining with her father. *Villette*

Animals in the Brontës

BLACK BESS: One of Huntingdon's horses. *The Tenant of Wildfell Hall*

CARLO: St. John Rivers' pointer. *Jane Eyre*

CHARLIE: Catherine Linton's pointer, bitten by the Wuthering Heights dogs on her first visit there. *Wuthering Heights*

FANNY: Isabella Linton's springer, almost hung to death by Heathcliff. *Wuthering Heights*

GNASHER: A guard-dog at Wuthering Heights. *Wuthering Heights*

GREY TOM: One of Huntingdon's horses. *The Tenant of Wildfell Hall*

GRIMALKIN: Lockwood's name for a brindled grey cat at Wuthering Heights. *Wuthering Heights*

JACK: Edward Crimsworth's vicious horse which he delights to master by force. *The Professor*

JUNO: A huge, liver-coloured bitch pointer, attacks Lockwood. *Wuthering Heights*

MESROUR: Mr. Rochester's black horse. *Jane Eyre*

MINNY: Catherine Linton's Galloway pony. *Wuthering Heights*

NIMROD: One of Huntingdon's horses. *The Tenant of Wildfell Hall*

PHOEBE: One of Sam Wynne's pointers, which when possibly infected with rabies, bites Shirley who secretly cauterises the wound herself. *Shirley*

PHOENIX: Catherine Linton's pointer, bitten by the Wuthering Heights dogs on her first visit there. *Wuthering Heights*

PILOT: Mr. Rochester's Newfoundland dog, a lion-like creature with long black and white hair. *Jane Eyre*

RUBY: A horse ridden by Helen Huntingdon. *The Tenant of Wildfell Hall*

SANCHO: Gilbert Markham's beautiful black and white setter. *The Tenant of Wildfell Hall*

SKULKER: Old Mr. Linton's bull-dog, attacks Catherine Earnshaw. *Wuthering Heights*

SNAP: A little rough terrier, at first Matilda Murray's, later passes via the rat-catcher to Mr. Weston. *Agnes Grey*

SYLVIE: A small dog living in Mme. Beck's school, attaches herself especially to Paul Emanuel. *Villette*

TARTAR: Shirley's black-muzzled dog. *Shirley*

THROTTLER: A guard-dog at Wuthering Heights. *Wuthering Heights*

WOLF: A guard-dog at Wuthering Heights. *Wuthering Heights*

YORKE: Victor Crimsworth's mastiff, is bitten by a rabid dog and has to be shot. *The Professor*

ZOE: Shirley's mare. *Shirley*

Animals in Jane Austen

FOLLY: Sir John Middleton's pointer, one of whose puppies is promised to Willoughby. *Sense and Sensibility*

The Characters – Book by Book

Agnes Grey

ANNE BRONTE

Mansfield Park (cont.)

JANE AUSTEN

Northanger Abbey

JANE AUSTEN

Villette (cont.)

Wilson, Mr.   ^{Chapter} 8

Z——, M.   ^{Chapter} 27

Wuthering Heights

	Chapter
Archer, Dame	8
Branderham, Jabes	3
Dean, Ellen (Nelly)	4
Earnshaw, Mr.	4
Earnshaw, Mrs.	4
Earnshaw, Catherine	3
Earnshaw, Mrs. Frances	3
Earnshaw, Hareton	1
Earnshaw, Hareton	8
Earnshaw, Heathcliff	4
Earnshaw, Hindley	4
Fanny	12
Green, Mr.	28
Heathcliff	1
Heathcliff, Mrs. Catherine	
(*see* Linton, Catherine)	
Heathcliff, Linton	4
Heathcliff, Mrs. Isabella	
(*see* Linton, Isabella)	

	Chapter
Housekeeper	18
Jenny	6
John	6
Joseph	1
Kenneth, Dr.	8
Linton, Mr.	6
Linton, Mrs. Mary	6
Linton, Mrs. Catherine	
(*see* Earnshaw, Catherine)	
Linton, Catherine	2
Linton, Edgar	4
Linton, Isabella	6
Lockwood, Mr.	1
Mary	12
Michael	24
Robert	6
Shielders	6
Zillah	2